VOLUME TWENTY

Book One
COMMUNITY DEVELOPMENT AND RATIONAL CHOICE:
A KOREAN STUDY
John E. Turner, et al.

Book Two
CONFLICT PROCESSES AND THE BREAKDOWN OF
INTERNATIONAL SYSTEMS
Merriam Seminar Series on Research Frontiers
Dina A. Zinnes, Editor

CONFLICT PROCESSES AND THE BREAKDOWN OF INTERNATIONAL SYSTEMS
MERRIAM SEMINAR SERIES ON RESEARCH FRONTIERS

Dina A. Zinnes
Editor

Volume 20
Book 2

MONOGRAPH SERIES IN WORLD AFFAIRS

Graduate School of International Studies
University of Denver
Denver, Colorado 80208

Library of Congress Cataloging in Publication Data
Main entry under title:

Conflict processes and the breakdown of international systems.

(Monograph series in world affairs; v. 20, bk. 2)
(Merriam seminars on research frontiers in international and cross
national politics series; v. 1)
Bibliography: p.
1. International relations—Research. 2. International Relations—
Mathematical models. I. Zinnes, Dina A. II. Series. III. Series:
Merriam seminars on research frontiers in international and cross
national politics; v. 1.
JX1291.C625   1984   327   83-25338
ISBN 0-87940-073-0

ABOUT THE AUTHORS

DINA A. ZINNES became Merriam Professor in Political Science at the University of Illinois, Urbana, in 1980. Dr. Zinnes, who earned her Ph.D. at Stanford University in 1963, is a specialist in quantitative international politics and mathematical modeling. She is managing editor of the *American Political Science Review.* Her publications include: *Contemporary Research in International Relations: A Perspective and Critical Appraisal* (Free Press, 1976); *Mathematical Models in International Relations Research* (Praeger, 1977); and articles in journals such as *Comparative Political Studies, International Studies Quarterly, Journal of Conflict Resolution, Journal of Peace Science, Behavioral Science, World Politics,* and *UMAP Modules.*

CLAUDIO CIOFFI-REVILLA is Assistant Professor of Political Science at the University of Illinois, Urbana, where he was George A. Miller Visiting Scholar in 1981-82. He holds doctoral degrees from the "Cesare Alfieri" School of Political Science of the University of Florence, Italy, and from the State University of New York at Buffalo. He has published scientific papers on the application of mathematical models in the areas of strategic analysis, international communication, and the European Community. He is currently developing models, methods and applications of Political Reliability Theory in International Relations. In 1983 he was elected to membership in the International Medici Academy for his research on mathematical models of international conflict.

BRUCE BUENO de MESQUITA is Professor and Chairman at the Department of Political Science at the University of Rochester. A former Guggenheim fellow, he is the author of three books (the most recent of which is *The War Trap)* and numerous articles on international conflict, coalition theory, and politics in India. His current research focuses on the application of expected utility theory to the initiation, escalation, and termination of international conflict. He is completing a book on the advancement of American national security interests while avoiding military intervention.

MANUS I. MIDLARSKY is Director of the Center for International Relations, and Professor of Political Science at the University of Colorado, Boulder. He is the author of *On War: Political Violence in the International System,* and of articles on international relations and conflict behavior which have appeared in journals such as the *American Political Science Review, American Journal of Political Science, Journal of Conflict Resolution, International Studies Quarterly* and *Polity.* His current research is funded by the National Science Foundation and the National Endowment for the Humanities. He is listed in *Who's Who in America.*

EDWARD E. AZAR is Professor of International Relations in the Department of Government and Politics, and Director of the Center for International Development at the University of Maryland, College Park. An international authority on the quantitative analysis of international events and conflict resolution, Professor Azar has written dozens of scientific articles and has written and edited a half dozen monographs, books and special journal issues on theory and methods of events data analysis, conflict behavior in the Middle East and the linkages between conflict and underdevelopment in the Third World. He has developed a major events data bank, the Conflict and Peace Data Bank (COPDAB), and has managed several major research projects on conflict images and the normalization of relations in the Middle East. Professor Azar is editor of the quarterly journal, *International Interactions.*

PHILIP A. SCHRODT is Associate Professor of Political Science at Northwestern University, where he teaches international relations, mathematical modeling, and environmental politics. He received a B.A. and an M.A. in Mathematics from Indiana University, and a Ph.D. in Political Science from the same institution. He has published numerous articles on applications of mathematical modeling to international relations and on the problems of statistically estimating nonlinear mathematical models. His current research deals with arms transfers, the applications of microcomputers to Political Science, and mathematical models of chaotic behavior.

TABLE OF CONTENTS

Conflict Processes and the
Breakdown of International Systems
Merriam Seminar Series on Research Frontiers

PREFACE

This volume is the first in the *Merriam Seminars on Research Frontiers in International and Cross National Politics Series.* Political Science researchers have ample opportunity to present papers at regional, national and international meetings. But although these meetings schedule formal discussants and reserve some time for response from the floor, they typically do not provide an adequate forum to test out, challenge, or probe basic research questions. The Merriam Seminars furnish this opportunity.

The Seminars seek to bring together researchers who are involved in relatively comparable areas of inquiry to explore in considerable depth a limited number of topics. A typical seminar consists of two days of presentations together with exhaustive, yet positive and informal, question-and-answer discussions. The area of quantitative international politics has too frequently seen one researcher undercut another. The purpose of the Merriam Seminars is to provide a critical but supportive atmosphere for the encouragement and enhancement of subsequent work.

A key attribute of the Merriam Seminars, then, is intensive, informal, and positive examination of a set of related research questions. A second characteristic is that the research presented is at the forefront in the field of International Politics. The Seminars focus on research projects that employ some of the most advanced methodological tools and some of the lesser known but useful mathematical languages. Thus the Seminars not only consider major questions of the field, but do so in an imaginative and creative fashion.

Finally, but by no means least, the Merriam Seminars provide a component of graduate training. Several sessions of each Seminar are specifically set aside for the presentation of advanced graduate student research proposals. These sessions provide the students with an opportunity to expose their ideas to a larger community and receive feedback from research scholars outside their own institutions. The graduate students who attend the Seminars are drawn, for economical reasons, from within a small radius of the University of Illinois campus, where the Seminars are held twice each year. However, the invited research scholars are also encouraged to bring with them one or two advanced graduate students. This practice not only directly benefits the research projects of the students making the presentations, but also those who attend the Seminars to gain insight into both the profession and their own projects.

Thus the University of Illinois Merriam Seminars seek to bring together major researchers asking questions in creative new ways, and to provide an avenue for graduate student training by actively involving a select number of graduate students.

Future publications resulting from these sessions will combine relevant sets of papers from several of these seminars in order to make them available to the research community. These articles will be grouped around a general research problem and the authors are asked to revise the papers in light of subsequent discussions. The entire volume is subject to external review. It is our intention that information gained in the Merriam Seminars can be shared with the wider research community through these volumes.

INTRODUCTION

Dina A. Zinnes

This volume of the Merriam Seminar Series focuses on the problem of system breakdown or collapse. In the opening chapter Cioffi provides a general model for the study of system breakdown. The remaining chapters concern a very special form of international system collapse: violent conflict and its escalation into war. The articles differ in terms of the level at which the problem is analyzed—intra-nation and inter-nation—and with respect to the specific component of the process that is singled out for consideration, whether it is the decision-making process, alliance configurations, or hostility interaction patterns. They also represent a diversity in modeling approaches: an expected utility theory, probability theory, differential and difference equation models. These differences in level of analysis, system breakdown focus and modeling approach provide us with an exciting and multifaceted exploration into the whys and wherefores of the collapse of international systems.

In "Political Reliability In International Relations" Cioffi outlines a general theory of system collapse. The theory is based on a consideration of the components of any general political structure and the determination of the reliability probability of each component. Cioffi shows that if a structure can be decomposed into a set of independent elements, the overall reliability of the entire structure is a multiplicative function of the individual reliabilities. Consequently, the reliability of the total structure involves an interplay between the probability of each component part and the number of such parts. Because the total reliability of a structure is not a simple linear function of the individual reliabilities of the component parts, Cioffi demonstrates that the capacity of a political structure to survive, i.e., maintain itself, is typically quite different from what intuition might suggest. He shows how political structures with components that have high levels of reliability are frequently considerably less reliable than one might suspect.

Although Cioffi's argument is made principally in terms of political structures, it is not difficult to see how the theory generalizes to political processes. A set of interacting nations can be seen as a "structure" in which each individual nation is an independent component. The system's reliability, i.e., its propensity for self-maintenance, depends on the multiplicative probabilities that each nation behaves in certain ways. Thus, as Kaplan noted in *System and Process* (1957), the preservation of an international system depends on the extent to which its units accept and behave according to its rules. When this does not occur—or in Cioffi's terms, when a nation's propensity to behave according to the rules of the system decreases—then the total reliability of the system decreases, i.e., the potential for system collapse increases. Many, like Rosecrance (1963), have identified such system breakdowns as equivalent to war.

The question then becomes one of how these individual probabilities are determined. One answer is supplied in Chapter 2 by Bueno de Mesquita. "An Expected Utility Explanation of Conflict Escalation" presents a model of the decision calculus that national leaders use in determining when to escalate a conflict into violence. Using the model he initially laid out in *The War Trap* (1981), Bueno de Mesquita shows how an expected utility calculation can explain when a decision maker will escalate a conflict. The calculus involves an assessment of one nation's utility for another's overall policy together with an estimate of the likelihood of winning a conflict with that nation. By placing this decision calculus in various environments, Bueno de Mesquita can indicate a nation's propensity to engage in war. In effect, then, each nation's individual expected utility calculation provides an indication of its "reliability" within the broader international system context. While neither Cioffi nor Bueno de Mesquita provide the actual link between the expected utility calculation and the reliability of the component parts of the system, the correspondence between the two models makes such a suggestion obvious and intriguing.

A second and rather different answer to the question of how the individual probabilities are determined can be found in Chapter 3. Midlarsky's "Alliance Behavior and the Approach to World War I" is an analytical study of a specific system breakdown—the occurrence of World War I. But while the attempt is to understand the processes that produced a specific historical event, a specific systemic collapse, Midlarsky provides us with the basis for a more general theory of system collapse. The level of analysis remains the individual nation, but unlike the Bueno de Mesquita model, the focus is not on decision making. In one sense one might argue that the Midlarsky model assumes the decision calculus and now looks more broadly at the behavior of the national units. The Midlarsky model is concerned with a nation's general propensity to act in certain ways. The behavior of interest is that of alliance formation. Following the balance of power theory, Midlarsky's argument is that system maintenance, i.e., the reliability of a system, is a direct consequence of the extent to which the formation and dissolution of alliances is in equilibrium. When this occurs, the system is preserved; when it does not occur, as was the case prior to World War I, there is system breakdown.

Although the probabilities in the Midlarsky model are not the same as the probabilities in the Cioffi model, there is an implicit linkage between the two. The probabilities in the Cioffi model concern the probability that a nation will perform in certain ways. The probabilities in the Midlarsky model are that a given nation will form or dissolve an alliance. Nevertheless, while different, there is an obvious relationship between the two models: the propensity for a nation to behave according to certain rules is clearly related to the probability that nations will join or dissolve alliances. According to Kaplan, a critical ingredient in the functioning of the balance of power system is the willingness of the nations to abide by the rule that they form and dissolve alliances with impunity. The extent to which the nations of a system follow this rule will in turn determine the extent to which an equilibrium between alliance formation and dissolution is maintained.

"The Theory of Protracted Social Conflict and the Challenge of Transforming Conflict Situations" (Chapter 4) is not directly concerned with the issue of system breakdown. But this difference is more apparent than real. Azar points to an important but little-studied aspect of conflict processes: long-term conflicts that are essentially never solved or are only resolved over extremely long-time horizons, and that heat up and cool down at almost regular intervals. Azar seeks to identify the basic ingredients of protracted social conflicts and to indicate how they differ from other forms of conflict. Thus protracted social conflicts are not system breakdowns. Indeed, they have a special structure all their own and in the sense of system reliability they contain a hidden factor that enhances the system's capacity to survive. Azar implies that the routinization and establishment of rules which underlie a system of protracted conflict encapsulates the conflict process and thereby prevents the breakdown of the system. But while protracted conflicts have a special kind of immunity to system collapse, their immunity is not total. Thus understanding the special structure of protracted conflicts is critical for understanding the immunity mechanism: when and why some protracted conflicts eventuate in war, while others do not.

Schrodt's article attempts to answer this question. As such, it connects the Azar article with the rest of the volume. "A Model of Sporadic Conflict" explores the capabilities of a logistic differential equation model for describing sporadic occurrences of high levels of conflict as interspersed between low levels of conflict. The model assumes that nations are composed of two principal groups, those for whom an international conflict is beneficial and thus wish to see high levels of conflict between their country and others, and a second group that gains from low levels of international conflict and thus seeks to reduce the level of conflict between their country and others. The pressures exerted by these two groups are proportional to the actual level of conflict. An interesting characteristic of the model is the introduction of lag times, the length of time it takes each of the two groups to react to the ongoing level of conflict. Schrodt shows how lag time and the amount of pressure exerted by each group combine to produce the sporadic high levels of conflict and how random disturbances affect this relationship. Schrodt's analysis implies that at least one of the possible "immunity" factors in protracted conflicts is the lag time: as lags increase, the frequency with which protracted conflicts shoot off to high levels decreases; as lags increase, the amount of pressure that must be exerted by the two internal groups to increase high levels of conflict also increases.

The last chapter provides a different approach to the study of system breakdown. It proposes that crises and wars should be seen as the culmination of the interaction processes of a subsystem of nations. The explosive nature of the interactive behavior of the nations provides the clue and perhaps the explanation for the collapse of the system. Although the article attempts to build on earlier interactive models, it argues that previous analyses have not provided adequate models for the study of crises and war. "An Event Model of Conflict Interaction" proposes a system-based model which examines the chronological sequence of behaviors without regard to the initiator of the action, and includes a new variable of "time between events." This study is concerned with the reliability of an international system from the perspective of the structure of the interaction process. If the behavior of the interacting units conforms to a particular pattern, the system will maintain itself. As long as the behavior of the units remains within certain bounds, the system will persevere. When the interactions exceed bounds, i.e., when there is an escalation in activity, the international system collapses.

Thus where Cioffi, Bueno de Mesquita and Midlarsky examine the impact of the behavior of the individual units on the reliability of the total system—Cioffi more generally, Bueno de Mesquita in terms of individual decision calculi and Midlarsky with reference to alliance formation—Azar, Schrodt and Zinnes emphasize the significance of interactions for system maintenance. For Azar and Schrodt the interactions are largely within the polity, while for Zinnes they are between polities.

This volume, then, implicitly and explicitly addresses the problem of system collapse. The articles differ with respect to *how* system reliability is examined. They also provide intriguingly different models. Cioffi's general framework is based on fundamental laws of probability theory. Bueno de Mesquita's model rests on the more general expected utility model of decision making. Midlarsky's analysis utilizes the probabilistic models of the Poisson and the Negative Binomial. Schrodt's model of protracted conflict is based on a differential difference equation involving stochastic terms. Zinnes' model is a type of difference equation model, but uses the event rather than time as the implicit independent variable. Thus we have a series of articles that focus on different facets of system reliability using different analytical perspectives. It is hoped that this diversity in focus and approach will make for challenging reading and, will stimulate future research.

1

POLITICAL RELIABILITY IN INTERNATIONAL RELATIONS
Claudio Cioffi-Revilla

*The world is a stupendous machine, composed of innumerable
parts, each of which being a free agent, has a volition and action of
its own; and on this ground arises the difficulty of assuring success
in any enterprise depending on the volition of numerous agents. We
may set the machine in motion, and dispose every wheel to one certain end; but when it depends on the volition of any one wheel, and
the corresponding action of every wheel, the result is uncertain.*

Niccolò Machiavelli
The Prince 1513

INTRODUCTION

A significant number of empirical phenomena in politics derive their
relevance from the fact that they are affected by the likelihood of
breakdown, lest certain contingencies take place. This pervasive
possibility of breakdown, a recurring feature of political life, gives rise
to the question of *political reliability,* defined here as the likelihood of
correct functioning, or "things going well" in the polity.

Research reported in this paper was made possible in part through a grant from
the University Research Council of the University of North Carolina, Chapel
Hill. I am grateful to Diane Napolitano for her assistance and to the staff of the
Institute for Research in the Social Sciences of the University of North
Carolina. An earlier version of this paper was presented at the first Charles E.
Merriam Seminar in Mathematical International Relations at the invitation of
Professor Dina A. Zinnes. I am grateful to her and to the University of Illinois
for the opportunity to have presented and discussed this project, as well as to
Karen Feste, Millie Van Wyke, and an anonymous referee for many helpful
comments.

In the field of International Relations, the reliability of political processes, ranging from nuclear deterrence policy to diplomatic communications systems, is of central importance, since great costs are associated with the collapse of today's complex social systems. In some instances, such as strategic nuclear balance, the calculus of political reliability has acquired unprecedented significance.

Like all man-made systems, political systems can deteriorate, malfunction, and collapse. Since early Greek times, the focus in maintaining governability has been to prevent political erosion and breakdown. The ever-present possibility of failure in political systems and processes is especially interesting in the study of politics; it is the subject of analysis in the Theory of Political Reliability.

During the past decades considerable progress has resulted from the application of systemic approaches to the study of international politics. And while some research has been directed to analyzing the causes, correlates, and frequency of breakdowns, the problem of *reliability* in complex international and political systems and processes still awaits a theoretically and empirically-oriented systematic treatment.

This article presents the concept of political reliability as a useful framework for understanding international politics. It covers the following areas: (1) the context of political reliability in international relations; (2) the fundamental concepts, methods, and results of political reliability; (3) applications that suggest implications of the theory and processes in International Relations; and (4) a summary of important aspects of the political reliability approach.

POLITICAL RELIABILITY IN INTERNATIONAL RELATIONS

In International Relations, there is a large and important class of phenomena which owes much of its relevance to the characteristic that the political system may fail to work. This is the case, for example, in diplomatic negotiations, ententes, detentes, and alliances. The continued existence of these sytems and processes depends crucially upon the execution of a complex set of steps, events, subprocesses, or conditions, each of which, in turn, may or may not work. In negotiations many necessary conditions must be successfully resolved; in alliances many allies must provide support. The resulting aggregate reliability of these political systems and processes is vital but generally far from straightforward.

Numerous international events, processes, and even entire systems derive their importance almost exclusively from the fact that their collapse, degradation, or failure entails significant political consequences.

Several examples are: (a) nuclear deterrence, where the credibility of successful deterrence plays a central role; (b) diplomatic communications, where the appropriate, correct interpretation of political intentions through messages requires several conditions; (c) antiproliferation policy, where success depends on the capacity to deny the requirements necessary for proliferation; (d) relations with allies and coalitions, where it is vital to assure and maintain political support from many actors; and (e) "power projections," where it is necessary to design, deploy, and maintain a credible concerted system of worldwide infrastructures, in support of national capabilities, for the pursuit of political objectives.

Within this class of political problems the central factor is the reliability of the supporting political system or process. "Will it work"? becomes the key question. Will the nuclear strategy actually deter? Will the antiproliferation policy successfully prevent proliferation? Will the diplomatic communication channel convey messages with sufficient political fidelity? Will the allies provide support? Will power project successfully? In each case, it is the reliability of the sustaining system or process that is decisive. In each instance, political reliability vitally depends upon a certain number of necessary conditions or requirements.

The first elements of a political reliability approach were developed in connection with the problem of credibility in nuclear deterrence theory (Cioffi-Revilla, 1975, 1977, 1981a), and the problem of conveying political messages in a diplomatic communications channel (Cioffi-Revilla, 1979). Although previous research has not focused directly on a General Theory of Political Reliability per se, other clusters of research have dealt with topics partially related to this question. The work of Richardson (1941, 1945a, 1945b, 1960) on the outbreak of wars (see also Moyal, 1949; Weis, 1963; Horvath, 1968; and Horvath & Foster, 1963) can be viewed as a study on the breakdown of peace, and therefore concerned with reliability of the international system. However, this work was limited to only those models pertinent to the reliability of single individual processes (i.e., the peace-war process), and systems reliability was not examined. Wright (1965) and Deutsch (1978), in studying wars resulting from a series of consecutive crises, used the concept of "cumulative risk," which suggests a probabilistic structure akin to political reliability. Unfortunately, neither provides a subsequent treatment. Finally, Dumas (1975) discussed the gross probability of nuclear war as it results from the unsafe behavior of nuclear weapons systems. However, in explaining the ensuing "national insecurity," only an intuitive use of reliability is made without rigorous theoretical development.

Although these works touch upon several aspects related to political reliability in international relations, none focus on it as an organizing framework for political analysis or identify the common thread running through these problems, forming a clear class of empirical phenomena. A General Theory of Political Systems Reliability—a substantive topic meriting separate discussion—is outlined in the next section. It should be kept in mind that an important distinction is made between two separate, but related, types of problems in political reliability: component reliability and systems reliability. The former refers to the likelihood of a single, individual breakdown in a sub-process/subsystem; the latter refers to the overall reliability of a political system. Although the emphasis in this article is on systems reliability, the essential aspects of component reliability are also outlined.

MODELS AND METHODS

Political Reliability Theory focuses on the multiple-step structure of political processes, or on the multiple-component structure of political systems. The central characteristic of all reliability models is that the political reliability of the overall process or system is viewed as crucially dependent upon the likelihood that the required steps will take place, or that the necessary components (i.e., institutions, policies) will work. However, as will be shown, this dependence is generally neither straightforward nor linear. As a consequence, an interesting feature of political reliability analysis is that it can account for forms of system-level behavior which differ substantially from the behavior of components.

In the real world the complexity of political systems will vary greatly. As a result, the analysis of political reliability in any concrete case can be complicated. The following discussion proceeds from simple to more complex political situations in international relations. (For mathematical detail please see the technical works of Kaufman, Grouchko & Cruon, 1977; Roberts, 1964; Mann, Schafer & Singpurwalla, 1974). Necessary mathematical discourse to accurately describe key concepts here and to illustrate how these are useful in the applications are found in the Appendix. One advantage of the Theory of Political Reliability is that many of its central concepts—such as *breakdown, series, link, parallel,* and *redundancy*—conform quite closely to ordinary language usage.

14

In the Theory of Political Reliability, basic models refer to the analysis of simple political processes consisting of a linear "chain" of events, arranged as a "string" of components. For example, a negotiation sequence, or a conditional threat based on a number of contingencies, are both political processes which can be modeled as a number of steps. (A special and very important variant of this situation is when each step is conditional upon the previous step; this is called a Markov process and is not dealt with here.) The essence of all basic "chain" models is that a number of necessary, nonoverlapping events have to take place in order for the political process to succeed; otherwise the process fails. This is a vital substantive quality of these problems. Quite aside from their intrinsic importance, basic chain models of reliability are also important for the analysis of many more complex cases. First, the basic models are presented, and then three analytic methods will be demonstrated.

Basic "Chain" Model

Consider a simple political process in which two events, E_1 and E_2, take place (e.g., to sign and to ratify a treaty). If these two events are independent of each other, then the reliability (r) of the entire overall process can be modeled as the probability of *both* events taking place. (A treaty is not in force unless it is *both* signed and ratified.) Or,

$$r = p_1 p_2. \tag{1}$$

Moreover, assuming there exists some "average" probability (p) of these two events (or required steps) taking place, then the political reliability of the process can be expressed as

$$r = p^2. \tag{2}$$

Equations (1) and (2) predict the reliability of a simple two-step political process, or a two-component political system. An analysis of this first simple model will be given below.

Although two steps may be all that is required in many political processes in international relations (e.g., signature and ratification in the creation of a treaty), in most practical cases a more general model is desirable. Consider a political process in which m events—E_1, E_2, E_3, . . . , E_m—take place as in a chain (e.g., Webbe, 1980). If the m events are independent from one another, then, by mathematical induction, the political reliability (r) of the general chain model is

$$r = p_1 p_2 p_3 \ldots p_m. \tag{3}$$

(Note that the probabilities [p_i] must be independent.) As before, using the "average" probability (p) of these m required steps in the chain, then

$$r = p^c. \qquad\qquad 1 \leq c \leq m \tag{4}$$

In this general chain model (equation [4]), political reliability is a function of two variables: (a) mean, single-step performance, denoted by p; and (b) the complexity, or number of steps necessary to complete the entire process, denoted by c. In the sequel these two variables will be referred to as performance and complexity. Since the domains of p and c are (0,1) and (1, $+\infty$), respectively, the range of political reliability is in the closed interval (0,1). Quite clearly, the two-step model, as well as any finite-step model, is a special case of the general chain model.

Significant results follow from the basic chain model of political reliability. Some first principles which govern the reliability of basic political processes are explored briefly through an analysis of scenarios, systems analysis, and simulation.

Scenario analysis. Consider a simple political process consisting of six steps, or c = 6. Within this process, consider two scenarios: an optimistic one, and a random one (table 1).

TABLE 1. Reliability of a Six-Step Political Process

Scenario	Mean Step Performances P_1 P_2 P_3 P_4 P_5 P_6						Overall Political Reliability r
Optimistic	.90	.99	.89	.95	.90	.80	.61
Random[a]	.10	.09	.73	.25	.33	.76	$.4\times10^{-3}$

[a]Values generated from a table of random numbers.

16

In the optimistic scenario, the performance of all six steps is allowed to be very high. What is the resulting reliability of the political process? Intuition would seem to indicate that—from inspection of the individual, subprocess performance levels (p_1 through p_6)—one could expect a political reliability for the entire process around 90%. However, by applying equation (3), it can be seen that in spite of high levels of subprocess performance, the overall political reliability in this scenario is no better than 61%. This global effect occurs because whenever probabilistic components, such as political events, are coupled together, the result is nonlinear and hence counterintuitive.

How does reliability behave in a random political process? Table 1 shows that when political peformance is left to chance, the ensuing reliability can drop to less than 1 in 1,000. (This confirms Machiavelli's observation quoted at the beginning of this chapter!)

Clearly, the attainment of even moderate reliability in simple political processes is very difficult, even in an optimistic scenario. Is high reliability more easily attainable in other simple political processes? Table 2 illustrates the reliability of low-complexity political processes ($c \leq 8$) under a variety of performance scenarios. Low and high

TABLE 2. Reliability r of Low-Complexity Political Processes as a Function of Performance

Mean Step Performance p	Complexity c of the political process			
	c=2	c=4	c=6	c=8
0.1	0.01	$\sim 10^{-3}$	$\sim 10^{-6}$	$\sim 10^{-9}$
0.2	0.04	0.0016	0.00006	0.256×10^{-5}
0.3	0.09	0.0081	0.00073	0.656×10^{-4}
0.4	0.16	0.0256	0.00409	0.654×10^{-3}
0.5	0.25	0.0625	0.01573	0.151×10^{-2}
0.6	0.36	0.1296	0.04666	0.017
0.7	0.49	0.2400	0.11765	0.057
0.8	0.64	0.4090	0.26114	0.107
0.9	0.81	0.6550	0.53144	0.439
1.0	1.00	1.0000	1.00000	1.000

values of p correspond to pessimistic and optimistic scenarios, respectively. Once again, reliability is difficult to attain, even in optimistic performance scenarios. For example, when c = 6, the reliability of the political process is hardly better than .53, even when subprocess performances are up to a level of .90. (As will be discussed, this general unreliability propensity is an intrinsic feature of all threat and reward systems, including deterrence, compellence, and others.)

Reliability *can* be high in very optimistic performance scenarios, but only if complexity (c) is low, as shown in table 3. As before, reliability

TABLE 3. Political Reliability r for Optimistic and Very Optimistic Performance Scenarios

Complexity	Mean Step Performance			
c	p=.80	p=.90	p=.95	p=.99
1	.800	.900	.950	.990
2	.640	.810	.903	.980
3	.512	.729	.857	.970
4	.409	.656	.815	.961
5	.327	.590	.774	.951
6	.262	.531	.735	.941
7	.209	.478	.698	.932
8	.167	.430	.663	.923
9	.134	.387	.630	.914
10	.107	.349	.599	.904
11	.085	.314	.569	.895
12	.068	.282	.540	.886
13	.054	.254	.513	.877
14	.043	.229	.488	.869
15	.035	.206	.463	.860
16	.028	.185	.440	.851
17	.022	.167	.418	.843
18	.018	.150	.397	.835
19	.014	.135	.377	.826
20	.012	.122	.358	.818

drops as political complexity rises, particularly for less-than-very-optimistic scenarios. Reliability also declines as performance drops, but particularly for complex political processes.

Finally, which levels of performance are required for attaining preferred reliability scenarios? Table 4 shows how, in order to reach even medium (r = .50) and moderate (r = .80) reliability, far higher levels of political performance are required.

TABLE 4. Required Levels of Mean Step Performance p for Medium and Moderate Reliability

Complexity	Reliability	
c	r=.50	r=.80
1	.50	.80
2	.69	.89
4	.84	.95
6	.89	.96
8	.92	.97
10	.93	.98
15	.95	.99

Systems analysis. The preceding results were derived by numerical computation for some specific scenarios. At a more theoretical level, several other important implications follow from mathematical analysis of the general properties of simple reliability models. See figures 1 and 2.

FIGURE 1.   General Chain Model of Political
Reliability: Family of Parametric Functions
r(p,c)

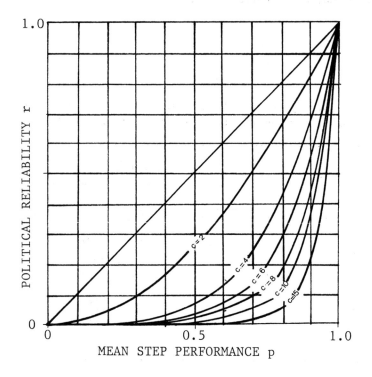

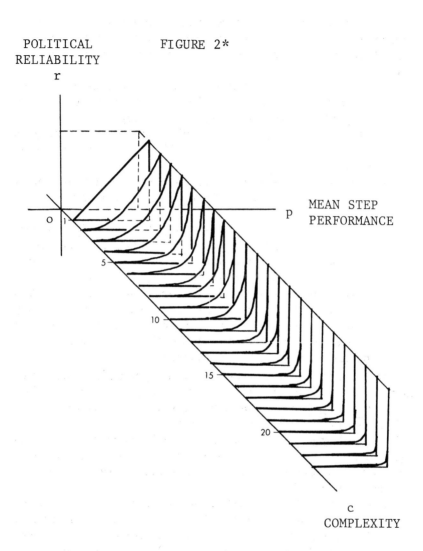

POLITICAL
RELIABILITY
r

FIGURE 2*

MEAN STEP
PERFORMANCE

c
COMPLEXITY

*General Chain Model of Political Reliability:
Family of Parametric Functions r(p,c) on the
Complexity Continuum

A number of important analytical results are summarized in the Appendix. From these analytical results it can be shown that the sensitivity of political reliability has a number of important properties, including these:

1. Changes in the performance (p) of steps or components, and changes in the level of complexity (c) affect the reliability of the political process in entirely different ways;
2. The sensitivity of political reliability with respect to a change in complexity is less intuitive than with respect to a variation in performance;
3. In political processes of increasing complexity, the addition of more steps beyond the first few has a declining effect on political reliability;
4. Above all, a systems analysis highlights the intrinsic vulnerability, or "fragility," of all chain-like political processes: *A drop in the performance of a single political step induces* (ipso facto) *a more than proportional drop in overall reliability. This nonlinear effect is greatest in highly complex political processes.* This propensity toward political degradation is very difficult to counter, but it is an intrinsic general property of all multiple-step political processes. (See Appendix for mathematical descriptions of these results.)

Two additional aspects of political reliability in basic models are of special interest. First, when performance is very high ($p \simeq 1$), reliability is practically unaffected by variations in complexity. Therefore, on the whole, reliability will be most sensitive to variations in performance. This general result obtains faster as complexity increases. As a consequence, in complex political processes (high c) the improvement of reliability is most effectively achieved by increasing performance—not by decreasing complexity.

Second, if some levels of performance are time-dependent, then the analysis of the dynamic function [r(t)] is of special interest. In general, while the performance at some steps may improve in time, it may also deteriorate. The dynamic analysis of the resulting time-varying reliability will yield the longitudinal "time path" of reliability. The shape of such a time path will depend on the parameters and the form of each time-dependent performance function [$p_i(t)$]. The approach outlined here therefore provides a general framework for the analysis of dynamic as well as static political reliability.

Simulation. When the political process under study becomes too complex and detailed for either direct scenario analysis or mathematical treatment, computer simulation methods can be used to derive the resulting reliability. For example, this is usually appropriate for the analysis of a large number of scenarios, or for the analysis of dynamic, time-dependent political processes. Figure 3 illustrates the evolution of political reliability in a process depending on five steps, each having a different time path. The likelihood of the first three declines "straight" with constant rate of deterioration over time; the fourth dips and then

FIGURE 3. Dynamic Political Reliability r(t) Resulting from Five Performance Inputs. (The Naive Estimate is the Average Resultant.)

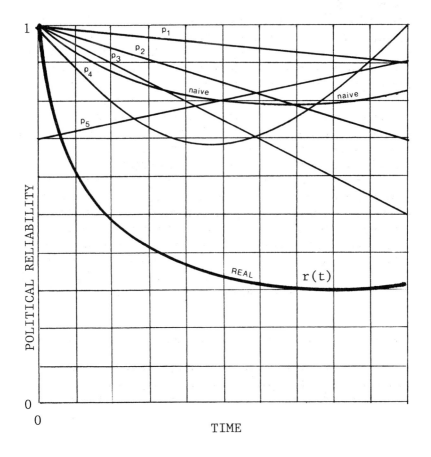

picks up to perfect performance; and the fifth rises constantly throughout. What is the resulting time-varying reliability of this political process? Computer simulations of such cases are very efficient since the analytical or numerical calculus can be lengthy, even when there is no technical challenge. In many complex cases, a computer simulation may be the only alternative, since the mathematical solution of many reliability functions is not tractable by analytic means. In the specific case at hand, it can be seen from the figure that the resulting time-varying reliability [r(t)] differs substantially from any of the component performance levels [(p$_i$(t)]. Various simulation "runs" with varying parameters of decay and improvement in component performance levels can be very helpful in shedding light on the dynamics of complex political systems.

Systems Models

The models presented thus far refer to the reliability of basic, simple political processes. In particular, these simple models view political behavior as resulting exclusively from a single, chain-like process. By contrast, in many empirical political situations one encounters a system of multiple redundant processes. This turns the focus of attention from the reliability of a single political process to a multi-process political system as a whole. To understand these more complex cases, two concepts are essential: series and parallel arrangements in the structure of political systems. (A useful physical model for understanding the following discussion is a set of Christmas tree lights.)

Series political structures. The basic structure of a political process consists of an ordered set of events—E_1, E_2, E_3, ..., E_m—as described by the general chain model. A political process can therefore be seen as having a "series" structure, since each event (E_i) is both necessary in order to carry out the process and independent of the other events.

Schematically, all chain models of political processes (equations [1] - [4] can be represented by the series diagram in figure 4. All models in the preceding analysis had this series structure. Although

FIGURE 4. Series Structure in a Basic Reliability Model

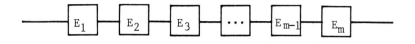

only marginally beneficial in the case of basic chain models, the schematic representation of reliability can be very useful in the case of more complex political systems.

Parallel political structure. Rather than relying on just a single process, many empirical political systems contain a variety of processes. These various component processes are said to be arranged "in parallel" when *all* of them must cease to function in order for the entire political system to cease functioning. A political system with parallel structure continues to operate even if only one component process is still functioning.

The reliability of a parallel-structure political system is more complex than that of a basic chain model. This greater complexity can be illustrated by examining a political system with two parallel processes sustaining it. From this simple case the reliability of a general system of parallel processes can then be inferred. This achieves two purposes: it explains the abundance of parallelism in politics; and it points to the concept of redundancy as a key variable for analyzing empirical political systems and explaining their behavior.

Consider a political system functioning on two parallel processes—P_1 and P_2. Imagine, for instance, an intelligence organization with two separate agencies. These are said to be in parallel because the political system ceases to function only when both processes cease to function. Because of its internal parallel arrangement, the reliability (R) of such a political system is not the same as in a basic chain process. Rather, if r_1 and r_2 denote the reliability of the individual parallel components, then the reliability of the overall political system is given by

$$R = 1 - (1-r_1)(1-r_2). \qquad (5)$$

This higher-order, systemic reliability is clearly different from that of a basic chain model, as shown by the schematic diagram in figure 5. (Compare figures 4 and 5.)

FIGURE 5.   Two Parallel Structures in a Political System

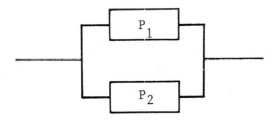

25

In turn, as shown in figure 6, the reliability of each individual subsystemic process can be modeled as a chain of events, each subprocess requiring yet another series of necessary steps. The political reliability of this five-component system is obtained by substituting

$$r_1 = p_{11}p_{12}p_{13} \qquad (6)$$

$$r_2 = p_{21}p_{22}$$

in equation (5), or

$$R = 1 - (1-p_{11}p_{12}p_{13})(1-p_{21}p_{22}). \qquad (7)$$

The reliability of parallel political structures has significant boundary properties. First, the political reliability of each parallel component cannot be greater than the weakest link in each chain; and in general, reliability will be weaker than the weakest link. Second, the reliability of the overall system is greater than the reliability of either component. The latter result, which is induced by redundancy, explains the propensity of many political systems to develop multiple parallel structures.

Political systems such as those in figures 5 and 6 suggest the theoretical possibility of a general political system composed of n parallel processes. Such a system has substantial empirical relevance, since many political systems are not limited to only two components.

The general expression for deriving the reliability of a political system of n parallel processes (each process consisting of a number of events) is obtained from expanding

$$R = 1 - (1-r_1)(1-r_2)(1-r_3) \ldots (1-r_n) \qquad (8)$$

to include the specific reliability of each process (i.e., the r_j's). In the special case in which all processes have the same reliability r, overall system reliability would then be

$$R = 1 - (1-r)^k. \qquad 1 \leq k \leq n. \qquad (9)$$

Analysis of these and other expressions for the reliability of general parallel political systems is not possible here. (See Appendix.) However, the theory yields a rich set of nonintuitive results, as the nonlinear form already predicts. For instance, the effect redundancy has on reliability is all but intuitively clear in complex, multi-process systems.

FIGURE 6. Internal Series Structure of Two Parallel Components in a Political System

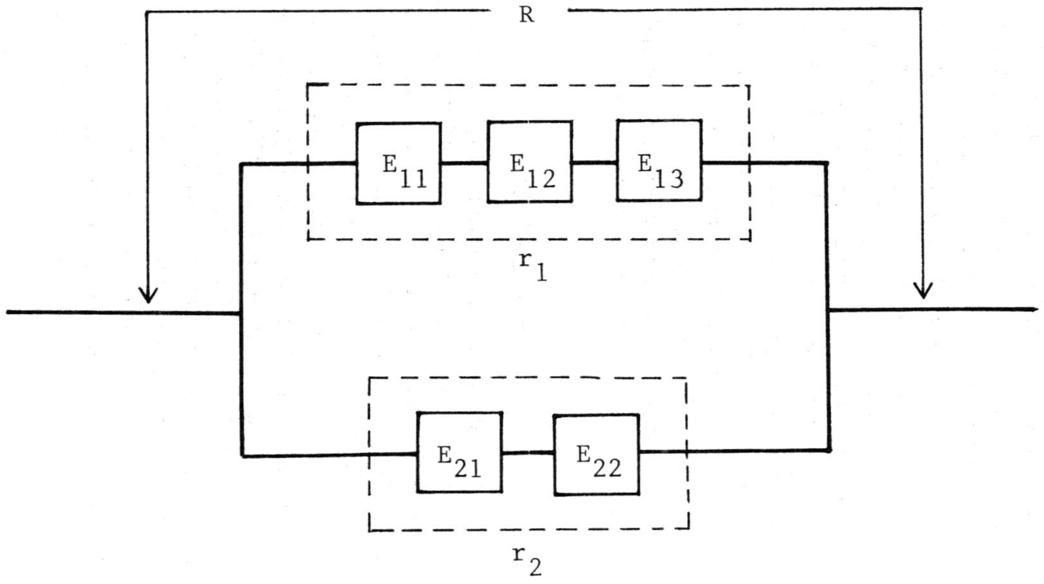

Mixed political structures. The discussion has thus far extended the concept of reliability to both series and parallel political systems. However, not much has been said about the reliability of systems having complex combinations of both serial and parallel arrangements. Examples of these mixed political systems are illustrated in figure 7.

The exact expression for the reliability of these mixed political systems is not examined here. (See Appendix.) However, attention should be paid to cases in which bottlenecks may act as limiting factors for the reliability of the entire political system. When this occurs, bottleneck components tend to have large internal redundancy, so that the reliability of the bottleneck component can be maximized and therefore its overall weakening effect minimized. Empirical political systems generally consist of a complex series/parallel arrangement of processes and events. When the structure of reliability is very complex, special procedures can be employed (Kouvatsos, 1976) in addition to the simulation methods already mentioned.

This concludes this section describing systems models of reliability and basic models. The next section provides an overview of some applications.

APPLICATIONS

Lewis Fry Richardson once observed that "engineers customarily learn the science of dynamics as a guide to the art of machine design. Unless statesmen have studied international dynamics, how can they expect their plans for peace to succeed?" (1960:xxxv). Something similar can be said about political reliability theory. In the following paragraphs several applications with special reference to international relations are discussed. [In-depth analyses of these implications are developed elsewhere (Cioffi-Revilla, 1979, 1981a, 1982a, 1982b, 1982c, 1983; Cioffi-Revilla and Merritt, 1982; Cioffi-Revilla and Zinnes, 1983).] Overall, the thesis is that if empirical political systems and structures are the result of social construction, then they should be subject to an analysis no less rigorous for reliability than their physical counterparts. Political systems should be analyzed for redundancy, vulnerability, failure rates, credibility, operational policy requirements, and systems complexity.

International Politics
The analysis of political reliability is relevant to both theory and policy in international relations. The systems approach is not new to international theory (see Kaplan, 1957; Boulding, 1962; Dougherty and

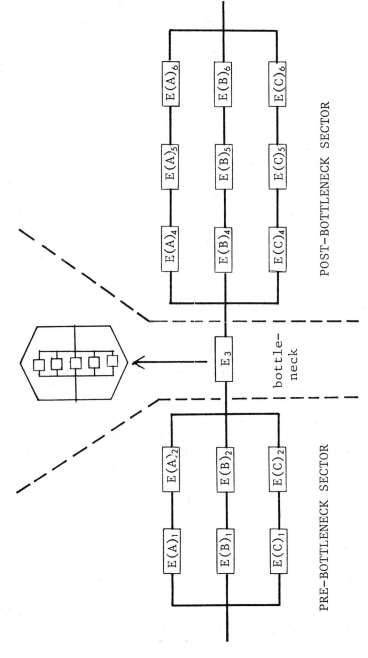

FIGURE 7. Mixed Structure with Internally Redundant "Bottleneck" Component

29

Pfaltzgraff, 1980:134-80). However, an approach that focuses on the political reliability of a broad set of systems and processes has not previously been applied. From the preceding outline it can be seen that the essential feature of these systems is an internal structure consisting of a number of events, processes, or institutions arranged in parallel and/or series configurations, each component being governed by a likelihood function. As noted earlier, a broad class of international systems possess these characteristics.

Political reliability is also of considerable importance from a foreign policy analysis perspective. Recent studies of policy planning in foreign affairs (e.g., Bloomfield, 1978) have reaffirmed the necessity for systematic planning. This is a particularly compelling conclusion in view of the irreversible dynamics of complexity and "hyperinteractivity" now at work in the international system (Scott, 1978). Moreover, the systemic performance of foreign political systems has traditionally been a central focus of diplomatic analysis. In a classical discussion of diplomacy, Nava (1955) describes how, as early as the seventeenth century, diplomats and analysts were required to master the art and science of "political arithmetick" (Petty, 1690). Current foreign policy analysis requires far more emphasis on political reliability aspects, given the increased stakes and high risks implicit in complex systems and processes in the mainstream of international relations (Diebold, 1966).

While several other applications in international relations can be suggested, six are of special interest: strategic deterrence, diplomatic communication, "power projection," nuclear proliferation, world order, and international conflict, negotiation, and war.

Strategic nuclear deterrence. Strategic deterrence theory occupies a prominent position among contemporary theories of International Relations (Dougherty and Pfaltzgraff, 1981; Ray, 1979; Coplin, 1980), since it explains the avoidance of war among rival nuclear powers. Deterrence theory is also important in strategic policy analysis; and in the area of general political theory it suggests a connection between conflict avoidance and the use of power (Schelling, 1966; Deutsch, 1978:23-32; Bell, 1975, 1979:205).

Deterrence means "preventing certain types of contingencies from arising . . . [by] communicat[ing] . . . to a prospective antagonist what is likely to happen to him should he create the contingency in question. The expectation is that, confronted with this prospect, he will be deterred from moving in directions that are regarded as inimical" (Kaufman, 1954:12). The credibility of the deterring threat is therefore vital, and it refers to "the extent to which a nation's threat to retaliate . . . is believable" (Pruitt and Snyder, 1969:107).

In spite of this theoretical recognition, the credibility of deterrence has yet to be treated directly and explicitly. Political reliability models can be used to analyze the credibility of deterrence policies since they necessarily implement a series of events that lead to a retaliatory strike. Classical deterrence theorists, such as Brodie (1946:76) and Wohlstetter (1959:216), have noted a multiple-step structure in the deterring process. Each event in a deterring process is subject to some likelihood, and the resulting credibility is a function of the reliability of this multiple-step process. This means that the credibility of retaliation—the core of deterrence systems—is governed by the patterns and principles outlined above. Moreover, the approach of political reliability theory also permits the analysis of topics such as the parallelism of the three-legged "nuclear triad" system, the effects of increased redundancy (MX, B-1, Trident weapons system), "nuclear sufficiency," and the dynamic evolution of credibility in time (e.g., detection of "windows").

Politico-diplomatic communication. The ability to secure and maintain efficient politico-diplomatic channels of communication is becoming increasingly urgent. Like other forms of social communication, politico-diplomatic communication transmits political signals (Cioffi-Revilla, 1979; Cioffi-Revilla and Merritt, 1982) by an encoding process that translates intended political messages (e.g., "firmness") into transmittable diplomatic signals (e.g., troop movement). These in turn are received by the target and decoded into perceived political messages.

In practice, diplomatic communication requires at least five steps: encoding, transmission, reception, noise filtering, and decoding. Because the basic channel has a chain-like structure (Shannon and Weaver, 1949), the reliability of politico-diplomatic communication is given by the familiar expression $R = r_1 r_2 r_3 r_4 r_5$. One nonobvious result is that a drop in the efficiency of any subcomponent of a diplomatic channel (e.g., encoding) induces a more than proportional drop in the overall reliability of diplomatic communication. From this, the necessity for multiple coding and multiple signaling clearly follows.

The above models are useful for the analysis and design of complex diplomatic communications systems. For instance, it can be shown (Cioffi-Revilla, 1979:238-40) that the use of third-party mediators induces a drop in the reliability of communication. This drop can be calculated, and the trade-offs to face-to-face communication compared

31

to show that the advantages of direct communication and negotiation generally far exceed whatever face might be saved by using mediators.

Power projection. The concept of power projection (Thompson, 1978) describes the ability to influence events by using foreign-based points of support to maintain an influence system of foreign bases, as well as maintain political ties with friendly political actors. Insofar as the entire arrangement of power projection depends on a chain-like configuration, the political reliability of the projection system is subject to the constraints and dynamics of series/parallel structures. This includes all multiple-step, politico-military operations (Webbe, 1980), as well as standing systems. Parallel alliances, redundant bases, and other elements which increase parallelism are the only basic strategies for containing the tendency of the overall arrangement to have a low political reliability. [Nettle (1980) discusses a NATO problem of wartime reinforcement which is typical of complex operations reliability.] This approach is not only useful in planning alternative configurations of power-projecting systems, but it also allows for a systematic analysis of rival systems which are perceived as threats. In particular, unduly high reliability (credibility) may be attributed to rival power projection systems which, on close analysis, turn out to have low overall system reliability.

Nuclear proliferation. The proliferation of nuclear weapons in the international system has been recognized as one of the most destabilizing processes currently taking place (Epstein, 1976; Cioffi-Revilla, 1978). Nuclear proliferation can be viewed as a chain-type process requiring access to weapons-grade materials, nuclear weapons engineering know-how, delivery systems, and politico-strategic necessity (or security motivation). In this chain model of proliferation, the *a priori* probability of proliferation can be predicted from the product of the four likelihoods corresponding to each of the four requirements. One result of taking this perspective is that it is sufficient to weaken only one of the required links in order to induce a more than proportional drop in the overall likelihood of proliferation. (Because of the small number of requirements, the function decreases very rapidly.) Therefore, the ability to deny any of the four events can achieve a significant antiproliferation effect. However, an efficient antiproliferation policy should consist of a parallel set of programs that will attempt to reduce each probability separately, thereby boosting the redundancy of the policy itself. For instance, reduction to an average likelihood of 80 percent in the above four requirements yields an overall probability of proliferation of barely 41 percent.

As time passes, however, it is clear that the probability of achieving certain requirements might change. The analysis of such changes implies many dynamic probability considerations. Making various assumptions about future component probability trajectories, the evolution of P(t) describes the future proliferation potential. Analysis of this type may reveal optimal periods in time for which the chance of successful antiproliferation policies can be calculated.

World order. The problem of world order can be seen as a political reliability problem from two separate perspectives—the political reliability of national level foreign policy and of global policies.

From a foreign policy perspective, political reliability is vital since it refers to the probability of achieving intended political goals. Every foreign policy is, from the framework of political reliability analysis, a configuration of parallel programs, with each program being carried out by a series of operations. For instance, a policy of development generally consists of a multiple-pronged approach comprising economic aid, military assistance, technology transfer, cultural exchange, and other aspects. Some of these programs are arranged in parallel structures (often the organization of the project itself specifies this); some others are in series. Political reliability analysis is therefore a heuristic framework for foreign policy analysis when viewed from this perspective. It is useful for describing, analyzing, and predicting the structure of probable success and failure in foreign policy.

The analysis of political reliability in international systems yields some significant insights for the construction, maintenance, and stability of world order and alternative world futures. In essence, the reliability of world order can be said to depend on the functioning of political organizations and processes. The functioning of world order components (Lazslo, 1974) aggregates according to the models presented above. In general, world order gains in reliability when parallel efforts and/or institutions are implemented. Redundancy is essential for the construction of an increasingly stable world order. Each institution carries out functions by chain-like processes, so their redundancy must increase in order for the resulting reliability not to decline. Monitoring the stability of world order, from this perspective, means monitoring the state of the reliability which results from the complex structure of parallel and/or series components of the global system. Peacekeeping operations—a microcosm of world order—can be planned and viewed in this light.

Conflict, negotiation, and war. Insofar as credibility and reliability mean higher or lower levels of political uncertainty in the international environment, the analysis of political reliability links naturally to the analysis of conflict. Moreover, foreign policy reliability also relates to the analysis of negotiations, since negotiation (Ikle & Leites, 1962) is a process of modifying utilities. Assuming that negotiation behavior is governed by expected utility, it can be argued that it is just as important to modify the probability of utility as the utility itself. This probability is obviously related to political reliability and credibility. From this perspective, bargaining is also a process of modifying credibility, and is subject to the models already outlined. In turn, the outcome of negotiations—primarily treaties—generates a network of norms (ACDA, 1980; Pampaloni, 1965) which can be analyzed for their political reliability. Conflict and war, from this perspective, can refer to the "breakdown" of peace systems (Cioffi-Revilla, 1982b; Cioffi-Revilla and Zinnes, 1983). As Wright (1965:272) noted, the probability of war over a period of crises is given by one minus the probability of avoiding war during the period. Since this argument is isomorphic to a system of parallel structures (one for each crisis), the concept of political reliability links directly to Wright's theory of war.

General Politics

In the current political environment of high risk, low controllability, great uncertainty, and increasingly stressful environmental conditions, the analysis of political reliability may no longer be a luxury. Just as it is no longer acceptable to design, build, and operate an advanced engineering project (such as a drawbridge or a spacecraft) without an *a priori* reliability assessment, it is now unacceptable to design, build, and operate large socio-political systems without any idea of their reliability under a set of likely environment conditions, including shock (oil embargo), deterioration (inflation), or prolonged attrition (conflict, unemployment, crime, terrorism). If politics is the art of the possible (de Jouvenel, 1963), then the reliability of political systems is a useful concept for the analysis of politics.

Beyond the international applications just suggested, it is possible to envision other areas of applicability in general political systems—international or domestic. In particular, the analysis of political reliability may become especially important for governments which are based on advanced socio-technological infrastructures for channeling their "nerves of government" (Wiener, 1961; Deutsch, 1964).

In general, political action consists of a complex array of parallel and/or chain-like goal-directed efforts. If a cybernetic model of government is employed for the political system (Deutsch, 1964;

Lazslo, 1974), then the requirements are a stable goal definition, information feedback, analysis, and course correction. The cybernetic model of politics yields an overall reliability of $R = r_1 r_2 r_3 r_4$, where each r refers to the reliability of components. In turn, each series component in a cybernetic model is composed of a parallel/series substructure down to the most basic and fundamental governmental operation.

Of the many possible applications, three seem particularly interesting: the stability of political coalitions, the reliability of political systems in general, and the systems reliability problem in political power management.

Political coalitions. Political coalitions are maintained by incentives or sidepayments (Riker, 1962); in most instances these incentives are numerous and simultaneous. As a consequence, the *cohesion* of a political coalition very often depends on the ability to ensure, with a very high level of probability, a number of benefits in return for support. The *reliability* of a coalition is therefore a function of the reliability of these incentives persisting over time. In effect, the political reliability of a coalition is a function of the reliability of these incentives persisting over time. Therefore, the political reliability of a coalition can be analogous to a system of parallel components (incentives), each of which has a substructure. This perspective is useful since it yields a measure of political reliability which is intuitively proportional to the stability of the coalition.

Another aspect refers to the number of allies. If allies in a coalition make decisions independently, then the alliance makes policy as a system of n parallel components. In practice, the number of required "yeas" is of course less than n, particularly for large n. (This explains why unanimity is absurd in large bodies—its reliability is practically nonexistent.)

Finally, the problem of coalition management can be seen as a problem of maintaining high reliability. In this sense, a theoretical connection exists between the analysis of political reliability on the one hand, and the theory of collective goods on the other. In particular, if some of the probabilities in alliance chain structures depend on allied performance, then such allies have an amount of "power" greater than whatever change they can control, since, by making its own performance drop, an ally can in fact induce more than a proportional drop in the overall alliance reliability. This political situation is akin to that of pivotal power, except that it results from an entirely different set of considerations.

Political security and evolution. The systems approach to politics and government has focused on the structure and functional processes which take place within political systems. Among the various central topics of political systems analysis has been the stability (or governability) of the system. In a cybernetic sense, political reliability refers to the security of the political system (or the probability of government). Political security, therefore, entails constant reliability analysis and maintenance of the polity, since, like all man-made systems, political systems can fail to function—along with their institutions, roles, and traditions.

Just as it is possible to conduct reliability diagnoses for the case of other man-made systems, it is possible to analyze the reliability of political systems by using statistical data on the political performance of institutions, organizations, and governmental functions. Moreover, from this perspective the process of political development consists of the growth of parallel political structures into complex systems having high redundancy. The distinction between parallel and series components is essential to understand the growth vs. development distinction. Growth can mean a mere increase in either dimension, whereas development results from a careful balance of parallelism and redundancy.

Finally, the analysis of political reliability also addresses the development and evolution of political systems in time. That is to say, if some form of probabilistic natural selection is at work in the history of political systems, would it not be the case that the most reliable (enduring) would be the most likely to survive? The theory of political reliability could be a starting point in a renewed understanding of political evolution.

Power management. Finally, the analysis of political reliability suggests that the art of government can be redefined as the monitoring and maintenance of high reliability in the policy sector. This is ensured by a sufficiently redundant number of "nerves of government," each of which is highly reliable in carrying out its functions. This viewpoint predicts, for example, that policy failures that are connected chain-like to other governmental actions tend to induce more than proportional damage to the political system as a whole. Hence as the length and difficulty of governmental operations grows, it is necessary to expand parallel structures. This expansion will not result in increased overall political reliability; it will merely maintain existing levels. For example, recent studies on maintaining governability (Crozier, Huntington & Watanuki, 1980) tend to obscure the fact that the reliability of government is the object of very complex analyses. Recent studies miss the complexity which results when, in advanced postindustrial polities, political components are arranged in an intricate mesh of parallel and series structures. The approach outlined here can be used for analyzing the political reliability of these complex political systems.

Two concrete examples illustrate the relevance of political reliability for power management. First, consider power management as carried out by means of political communication (Bell, 1975, 1979): "the speaker makes action or outcome Y contingent upon the performance of action X by the listener. X or Y may be positive or negative. Y is directly controlled by the speaker. Power statements include, therefore, most kinds of threats and promises" (Bell, 1975:205). Quite clearly, if power management is based on the execution of conditionals, then the reliability of that action, which is either threatened or promised, becomes the central question. If only a simple chain is implied, then the credibility (or reliability) of the power statement can be very fragile, as has been shown. If the target can weaken one link, the entire chain will lose more than proportional reliability. As a consequence, when the management of power consists of a network of commitments and agreements (Haselkorn, 1978), any complete analysis must include those reliability problems arising in any complex structure.

Finally, consider power management as a problem in designing an efficient, power-maintaining policy (Machiavelli). A reliability approach to this problem would suggest that the following must be estimated: (a) the probability of correct and timely problem identification; (b) the probability of correct political diagnosis; (c) the probability of correct means-ends calculus; (d) the probability of adequate resources; (e) the probability of successful implementation; and (f) the probability of avoiding self-destructing unintended consequences. The political reliability for this general system of power maintenance is the result of a six-component chain structure and is subject to laws of reliability deterioration discussed earlier. In particular, a small slip in the reliability of any of the six requirements of a power management policy will induce a more than proportional overall political deterioration. Therefore, power management must rest on several parallel reliable policies, and fluctuations in component reliability must be constantly monitored and restored. Power erodes quickly as each of the policy requirements becomes more and more difficult to maintain in an ever more complex world.

SUMMARY

Political reliability refers to the probability of desirable events and processes taking place in the political system. Political reliability depends not only on the likelihood that subprocesses and components will work, but, most crucially, it depends on the structural arrangement between the components of political system or process. Basically, three arrangements exist—series, parallel, and mixed—each of which entail totally different problems of political reliability. For example, series structures in politics have an intrinsic propensity to degrade even faster than the degradation of their component parts. This means that a drop in the expected performance of any event in a series political process induces *ipso facto* a larger drop in the overall reliability of the process.

In International Relations, at least four aspects can be noted about the Theory of Political Reliability. First, previous models of international behavior, including those which concern multiple-step processes (e.g., communication, negotiations), have not addressed directly the question of political reliability. The models presented here focus directly on the problem of political reliability and propose a framework which is theoretically and analytically fruitful.

Second, as mathematical theories, the preceding models have several advantages (Gillespie, 1976; Saaty, 1968; Zinnes, 1976). Primarily they have the capacity to generate results (by any of three approaches—scenarios, analysis, or simulation) which are usually neither intuitive nor straightforward. In particular, without these models and methods, the precise analysis of how political reliability deteriorates as a function of performance, complexity, and redundancy would not be possible. Reliability modeling can contribute to the further development of mathematical structures useful for political theory and research.

Third, as was suggested by the discussion of several applications (strategic deterrence, diplomatic communication, power projection), these models can be extended to the study of political reliability in vastly more complex international systems and processes. These extensions provide the framework for a General Theory of Political Reliability, since these models describe the fundamental units of many multiple-step political processes, or multiple-component political systems.

Finally, the approach suggested by these models is applicable to a variety of political phenomena. The theoretical progression—from international relations problems to general politics—logically suggests a new form of analysis for the complex political systems likely to prevail in the future.

BASIC FORMULAE FOR THE CALCULUS OF POLITICAL RELIABILITY

A. FORMULAE FOR BASIC MODELS OF POLITICAL RELIABILITY

1. The two-step model is

$$r = p_1 \cdot p_2 \, ,$$

or

$$r = p^2 \, ,$$

given some geometric mean probability $p = (p_1 \cdot p_2)^{\frac{1}{2}}$.

2. The general chain process model is

$$r = p_1 \cdot p_2 \cdot p_3 \cdot \ldots \cdot p_m = \prod_{i=1}^{m} p_i \, ,$$

or

$$r = p^c \, , \qquad\qquad (1 \leq c \leq m) \, ,$$

given some geometric mean probability $p = (\prod_{i=1}^{m} p_i)^{1/m}$.

B. SYSTEM ANALYSIS OF BASIC MODELS

1. Sensitivity (comparative statics) of political reliability:

$$\partial r / \partial p = c \cdot p^{c-1}$$
$$\partial r / \partial c = p^c \cdot \ln p$$
$$\partial^2 r / \partial p^2 = c(c-1) \cdot p^{c-2}$$
$$\partial^2 r / \partial c^2 = p^c \cdot (\ln p)$$
$$\partial^2 r / \partial p \partial c = \partial^2 r / \partial c \partial p \ [\text{sic!}]$$
$$= p^{c-1} \cdot (1 + c \cdot \ln p) \, .$$

Since $0 \leq p \leq 1$ and $1 \leq c < +\infty$, it also follows that: (a) $\partial r / \partial p$, $\partial^2 r / \partial p^2$, and $\partial^2 r / \partial c^2$ are positive, upward concave; while (b) $\partial r / \partial c$ and $\partial^2 r / \partial p \partial c$ are negative, downward concave (convex) functions. Hence, in agreement with the scenario analysis, political reliability can be increased by increasing performance, and additional requirements (steps) beyond the first few have a declining effect on political reliability.

2. Gradient of $r(p, c)$.

The equation

$$\nabla r = (\partial r/\partial p)\hat{e}_p + (\partial r/\partial c)\hat{e}_c \ ,$$

where $\hat{e}_p$ and $\hat{e}_c$ are unit vectors in dimensions p and c, respectively, describes the direction of greatest drop in political reliability. If $p \approx 1$, then $\partial r/\partial c \approx 0$, and therefore ∇r depends almost exclusively on $\partial r/\partial p$. Therefore,

$$\lim_{p \to 1} (\partial r/\partial p + \partial r/\partial c) = \partial r/\partial p$$
$$= c \cdot p^{c-1} \ .$$

This result obtains faster as complexity increases.

C. SYSTEMS MODELS OF POLITICAL RELIABILITY

1. The formula for the political reliability of a 2-parallel political system is

$$R = 1 - (1 - r_1) \cdot (1 - r_2) \ .$$

2. Boundary properties of political reliability systems:

$$r \leq \min(p_1, p_2, p_3, \ldots, p_m)$$
$$R \geq \max(r_1, r_2, r_3, \ldots, r_n) \ .$$

3. The formula for the political reliability of a generalized, n-parallel political system is

$$R = 1 - (1 - r_1) \cdot (1 - r_2) \cdot (1 - r_3) \cdot \ldots \cdot (1 - r_n)$$
$$= 1 - (1 - r)^k \ , \qquad\qquad (1 \leq k \leq n)$$

given some average component reliability r.

4. Equations for the political reliability of mixed systems are derived as follows. Consider the schematic diagram in Figure 7, which

models a mixed system with a "bottleneck". The first step is to aggregate by sets of series sectors, as follows:

$$R = r_1(\text{pre-bottleneck}) \cdot r_2(\text{bottleneck}) \cdot r_3(\text{post-bottleneck})$$
$$= r_1(E_1, E_2) \cdot r_2(E_3) \cdot r_3(E_4, E_5, E_6) .$$

Then, partial reliabilities are as follows

a. Pre-bottleneck sector r_1 :

$$r_1 = 1 - [1 - p(A_1) \cdot p(A_2)] \cdot [1 - p(B_1) \cdot p(B_2)] \cdot$$
$$\cdot [1 - p(C_1) \cdot p(C_2)] .$$

b. Bottleneck sector r_2 :

$$r_2 = 1 - (1 - p_3)^k ,$$

with internal k-redundancy at the bottleneck.

c. Post-bottleneck sector r_3 :

$$r_3 = 1 - [1 - p(A_4) \cdot p(A_5) \cdot p(A_6)] \cdot$$
$$\cdot [1 - p(B_4) \cdot p(B_5) \cdot p(B_6)] \cdot$$
$$\cdot [1 - p(C_4) \cdot p(C_5) \cdot p(C_6)] .$$

The equations which describe the overall political reliability of mixed systems can be analyzed by methods similar to those employed in the analysis of basic models. However, simulation methods are often more practical.

REFERENCES

ACDA [United States Arms Control and Disarmament Agency] 1980. *Arms Control and Disarmament Agreements*. Washington, D.C.: U.S. Government Printing Office. (ACDA Publication 105, August 1980, P.P. viii + 239.)

Bell, D. V. 1975. *Power, Influence and Authority*. New York: Oxford University Press.

_____. 1979. Political Linguistics and Political Research. *International Interactions* 6(3), November: 193-208.

Bloomfield, L. B. 1978. Planning Foreign Policy: Can It Be Done? *Political Science Quarterly* 93(3), Fall: 369-391.

Boulding, K. E. 1962. *Conflict and Defense*. New York: Harper.

Brodie, B. 1946. *The Absolute Weapon*. New York: Harcourt Press.

Cioffi-Revilla, C. 1975. *Teoria della deterrenza e stabilita diadica nelle Relazioni Internazionali*. Doctoral dissertation, "Cesare Alfieri" School of Political Science, University of Florence.

_____. 1977. Thoughts on Strategic Weapons. *Yearbook of the Canadian School of Peace Research*. Dundas, Ontario (PRI-D): 13-24.

_____. 1978. A Cusp Catastrophe Model of Nuclear Proliferation. *International Interactions* 4(3): 199-224.

_____. 1979. Diplomatic Communications Theory: Signals, Channels, Networks. *International Interactions* 6(3): 209-265.

_____. 1981. A Probability Model of Credibility in Strategic Nuclear Deterrence. Paper delivered at the Annual Convention of the International Studies Association, 18-20 March, Philadelphia.

_____. 1981. Statistics, Diplomacy, and Early Science in International Relations. Paper delivered at the XIth Annual Meeting of the North Carolina Political Science Association, Wilmington, N.C., 24 April.

_____. 1982a. The Reliability of European Political Cooperation (EPC). A Stochastic Model. Paper delivered at the Annual Convention of the International Studies Association, Cincinnati, 24-27 March, 1982.

_____. 1982b. Political Reliability Theory and War in the International System. Paper delivered at the Annual Meetings of the Midwest Political Science Association, Milwaukee, 28 April-1 May, 1982.

_____. 1982c. The Political Reliability of Italian Governments: An Exponential Model. *American Political Science Review* forthcoming.

_____. 1983. A Probability Model of Credibility: Analzying Strategic Nuclear Deterrence Systems. *Journal of Conflict Resolution* 27(1) March: 73-108.

_____ and Merritt, Richard L. 1982. Communications Research and the New World Information Order. *Journal of International Affairs* 35(2) Fall/Winter: 225-245.

_____ and Zinnes, Dina A. 1983. The Breakdown of Inter-Nation Relations: A Political Reliability Theory of International Crises. Paper delivered at the Annual Convention of the International Studies Association, Mexico City, March, 1983.

Coplin, W. D. 1980. *Introduction to International Politics.* Englewood Cliffs, NJ: Prentice Hall.

Crozier, M., Huntington, S. P., Watanuki, J. 1980. *The Crisis of Democracy.* New York: New York University Press.

de Jouvenel, B. 1963. *The Pure Theory of Politics.* New Haven, Conn.: Yale University Press.

Deutsch, K. W. 1964. *The Nerves of Government.* New York: Free Press.

_____. 1967. On the Concepts of Politics and Power. *Journal of International Affairs* 21(2):232-241.

_____. 1978. *The Analysis of International Relations.* Prentice Hall: Englewood Cliffs. Second edition.

Diebold, J. 1966. Computer, Program Management, and Foreign Affairs, *Foreign Affairs* 1966:125-134.

Dougherty, J. E. and Pfaltzgraff, R. L. 1981. *Contending Theories of International Relations.* Philadelphia: Lippincott.

Dumas, J. L. 1975. Systems Reliability and National Insecurity. *Papers of the Peace Science Society* (International)25:15-34.

Epstein, W. 1976. *The Last Chance.* New York: Free Press.

Gillespie, J.V. 1976. Why Mathematical Models? In *Mathematical Models in International Relations,* D. A. Zinnes & J. V. Gillespie, eds. New York: Praeger. 37-61.

Haselkorn, A. 1978. The Expanding Soviet Security Network, *Strategic Review* 6(3) Summer:62-73.

Horvath, W. J. 1968. A Statistical Model for the Duration of Wars and Strikes. *Behavioral Science* 13(1) January:18-28.

_____ and Foster, C. C. 1963. Stochastic Models of War Alliances. *Journal of Conflict Resolution* 7(2) June 1963:110-116.

Ikle, C. F. and Leites, N. 1962. Political Negotiations as a Process of Modifying Utilities. *Journal of Conflict Resolution* 6(1) March:19-28.

Kaplan, M. A. 1957. *System and Process in International Politics:* New York: Wiley.

Kaufmann, W. W. 1954. *The Requirements of Deterrence.* Memorandum no. 7, Center for International Studies, Princeton University.

Kaufmann, A; Grouchko, D.; and Croun, R. 1977. *Mathematical Models for the Study of the Reliability of Systems.* New York: Academic Press.

Kouvatsos, D. D. 1976. Decomposition criteria for the design of complex systems. *International Journal of Systems Sciences* 7(10):1081-88.

Laszlo, E. 1974. *A Strategy for the Future*. New York: Braziller.

Mann, N. R., Schafer, R. E., and Singpurwalla, N. D. (1974). *Methods for Statistical Analysis of Reliability and Life Data*. New York: Wiley.

Midlarsky, M. I. 1974. Power, uncertainty, and the outset of international violence. *Journal of Conflict Resolution* 18(2) September:395-431.

Moyal, J. 1949. The distribution of wars in time. *Journal of the Royal Statistical Society,* Series A, 112(IV):446-449.

Nava, A. 1955. *Sistema della Diplomazia*. Rome: CEDAM.

Nettle, S. A. 1980. Civil Emergency planning and the reinforcement of Europe. *NATO Review* 28(2) April:29-33.

Pampaloni, G. 1965. I trattati stipulati dal Comune di Firenze nei secoli XII e XIII. *Archivio Storico Italiano* 123(448):480-523.

Petty, W. 1690. *Political Arithmetick*. London: Peacock & Hen.

Pruitt, D. G. and Snyder, R. C. 1969. *Theory and Research on the Causes of War*. Englewood Cliffs, N.J.: Prentice Hall.

Ray, J. L. 1979. *Global Politics*. Boston: Houghton Mifflin.

Richardson, F. L. 1941. Frequency of occurrence of wars and other fatal quarrels. *Nature* 148(3759) November 15:598.

————————. 1945. Distribution of wars in time. *Nature* 155(3942) May 19:610.

————————. 1945b. The distribution of wars in time. *Journal of the Royal Statistical Society* 107(III-IV):242-250.

————————. 1960. *Statistics of Deadly Quarrels*. Pittsburgh: Boxwood Press.

Riker, W. H. 1962. *The Theory of Political Coalitions*. New Haven: Yale University Press.

Roberts, N. H. 1964. *Mathematical Models in Reliability Engineering*. New York: McGraw-Hill.

Saaty, T. L. 1968. *Mathematical Models of Arms Control and Disarmament*. New York: Wiley.

Schelling, T. 1966. *The Strategy of Conflict*. Cambridge, Mass.: Harvard University Press.

————————. 1966. *Arms and Influence*. New Haven: Yale University Press.

Scott, A. 1978. The Logic of International Interaction. *International Studies Quarterly* 21(3) September:429-460.

Shannon, C. E., Weaver, W. 1949. *Mathematical Theory of Communication*. Urbana, Ill.: University of Illinois Press.

Thompson, W. S 1978. *Power Projection*. New York: National Strategy Information Center.

Webbe, S. 1980. Hostage-rescue mission's weak link. *Christian Science Monitor* 25 August:

Weiss, H. K. 1963. Stochastic models for the duration and magnitude of a 'deadly quarrel.' *Operations Research* 11(1) January-February:101-121.

Wiener, N. 1961. *Cybernetics.* Cambridge, Mass.: MIT Press.

Wohlstetter, A. 1959. The delicate balance of power. *Foreign Affairs* 38(1) January:211-234.

Wright, Q. 1965. *The Study of War,* 2nd ed. Chicago: University of Chicago Press.

Zinnes, D. A. 1976. *Contemporary Research in International Relations.* New York: Free Press.

2

AN EXPECTED UTILITY EXPLANATION OF CONFLICT ESCALATION: A PRELIMINARY ANALYSIS

Bruce Bueno de Mesquita

Leaders of nations resort to violence to achieve their objectives when a breakdown occurs in other means of conflict resolution. War, then, represents a failure by one or more nations to recognize the limits of their ability to extract benefits from adversaries. Thus, conflict occurs when a demand is made of another state—a demand which is either fulfilled, negotiated, or resisted. The initiating nation may be assumed to accompany its demands with some threat of reprisals if its demands are not met. The threats may be sincere or they may be bluffs. In this study, I argue that the escalation of conflict beyond a mere threat, so that it involves the actual use of violence, depends on the relative expected utilities of the initiator and the opponent. Unlike the initial decision to begin a conflict, in which one nation determines whether or not the event occurs (Bueno de Mesquita, 1980, 1981), the decision to escalate to a violent confrontation is the product of calculations by both sides. These calculations involve estimating whether resistance, negotiation, or capitulation is the most appropriate response to a threat-bearing demand.

Before turning to the calculations that may lead decision makers toward or away from violence, let me summarize the structure of the expected utility computations that I contend all rational expected utility calculating leaders make when contemplating conflict (Bueno de Mesquita, 1981). The theoretical structure summarized here has proven successful in accounting for the initiation, outcome, and intensity of conflict across a rather lengthy time span (1816-1974) and across a broad number of geopolitical contexts. Similar expected utility models have also been successful in accounting for third-party decisions to join one side or the other or to remain neutral during ongoing wars (Altfeld and

Bueno de Mesquita, 1979) and in accounting for national decisions to comply or defect from international treaty organizations (Berkowitz, 1981). This study, then, should be seen in the context both of an explanation of conflict escalation and in the context of an example of the cumulativeness of knowledge that seems to result from the expected utility perspective.

I assume national decisions to initiate or escalate conflict involve expected utility calculations across the following three lotteries:

$$E(U_i)_b = [P_i(U_{ii} - U_{ij}) + (1 - P_i)(U_{ij} - U_{ii})]_{t_0} + P_{i_{t_0}}[\Delta(U_{ii} - U_{ij})]_{t_n - t_0}$$

$$+ (1 - P_i)_{t_0}[\Delta(U_{ij} - U_{ii})]_{t_n - t_0} \qquad (1)$$

$$E(U_i)_{k_\ell 1} = [P_{ik_\ell}U_{ik_\ell i} + (1 - P_{ik_\ell})U_{ik_\ell j}]_{t_0} + P_{ik_{\ell_{t_0}}}(\Delta U_{ik_\ell i})_{t_n - t_0}$$

$$+ (1 - P_{ik_\ell})_{t_0}(\Delta U_{ik_\ell j})_{t_n - t_0} \qquad (2)$$

and

$$E(U_i)_{k_\ell}2 = [(1 - P_{jk_\ell})U_{ik_\ell i} + P_{jk_\ell}U_{ik_\ell j}]_{t_0} + (1 - P_{jk_\ell})_{t_0}(\Delta U_{ik_\ell i})_{t_n - t_0}$$

$$+ P_{jk_{\ell_{t_0}}}(\Delta U_{ik_\ell j})_{t_n - t_0} \qquad (3)$$

Where

i = a nation contemplating the initiation of a conflict.

j = the nation against which i is contemplating the initiation of a conflict.

k_ℓ = some third-party nation.

U_{ii} = i's utility for i's most preferred policy portfolio. $U_{ii} = 1$ by definition.

U_{ij} = i's utility for j's policy portfolio. U_{ij} varies between $+1$ and -1.

$(U_{ii} - U_{ij})_{t_0}$ = i's perception of the potential benefits from succeeding in a bilateral conflict with j in which i can then impose new policies on j. This term reflects i's current evaluation of the difference between i's current policies and i's perception of j's current policies (hence it is evaluated at time t_0.) Thus, the greater the perceived similarity between i's current policies and j's current policies, the less utility i expects to derive from altering j's policies.

$(U_{ij} - U_{ii})_{t_0}$ = i's perception of the potential costs resulting from losing a bilateral contest with j, after which j can impose new policies on i. This term reflects i's current evaluation of how much j could shift i's policies to make them more in line with j's interests as perceived by i.

P_i = i's current perception of the probability of winning a bilateral conflict with j.

$1 - P_i$ = i's current perception of the probability of losing a bilateral conflict with j.

$U_{ik_\varrho i}$ = i's perception of the utility to be derived from each third party k_ϱ.

$U_{ik_\varrho j}$ = i's perception of the utility to be derived by j from each third party.

P_{ik_ϱ} = i's perception of his probability of success against j, given that third parties k_ϱ aid i.

$1 - P_{ik_\varrho}$ = i's perception of his probability of failing against j, given that third parties k_ϱ aid i.

P_{jk_ϱ} = i's perception of his probability of losing to j, given that third parties k_ϱ aid j.

$1 - P_{jk_\varrho}$ = i's perception of his probability of defeating j, given that third parties k_ϱ aid j.

$\Delta (U_{ii} - U_{ij})_{t_n - t_0}$ = i's perception of anticipated change in the difference between i's policies and j's policies over the time period t_0 to some future time t_n.

$\Delta (U_{ij} - U_{ii})_{t_n - t_0}$ = i's perception of anticipated change in how much j would want to alter i's policies in the future compared to j's current perceived policy differences with i. This term represents i's perception of anticipated future potential policy losses to j, while the previous term represents i's perception of future potential policy gains to be derived from imposing i's will on j. Both this and the previous term represent i's estimates under the assumption of no war.

$\Delta U_{ik_\varrho i t_n - t_0}$ = i's perception of anticipated future changes in the utility i can expect to derive from the assistance of k_ϱ.

$\Delta U_{ik_\ell jt_n - t_0}$ = i's perception of anticipated future changes in the utility j can expect to derive from the assistance of k_ℓ.

t_0 = the time at which i is calculating expected utility. Any term with this subscript is computed based on current values.

$t_n - t_0$ = the time span over which i estimates expected changes in utility values.

$E(U_i)_b$ = i's expected utility from a bilateral conflict with j.

$E(U_i)_{k_\ell}1$ = i's expected utility from a multilateral conflict with j in which k_ℓ is viewed as supporting i.

$E(U_i)_{k_\ell}2$ = i's expected utility from a multilateral conflict with j in which k_ℓ is viewed as supporting j.

Since the two multilateral lotteries entertain the possibility that some third parties can try to help or hinder both i and j (i.e., $U_{ik_\ell}i$ and $U_{ik_\ell}j$ can be greater than, less than, or equal to zero), i is interested in the net— not gross—contribution to be expected from each such third party. Consequently, the overall expected utility derived from third parties (hereafter $E(U_i)_{k_\ell}$ is:

$$\sum_{\ell=1}^{5} E(U_i)_{k_\ell} = \sum_{\ell=1}^{5} E(U_i)_{k_\ell}1 - \sum_{\ell=1}^{5} E(U_i)_{k_\ell}2 \tag{4}$$

where there are five types or sets of third-party nations, characterized by differences in the signs of their utility terms, and differences in the net value of the utility terms with i and with j.

Letting $E(U_i)$ represent i's overall expected utility from initiating a conflict with j, I can now define the minimal expected utility decision rules for risk-acceptant and risk-averse actors, whether making choices in an environment that is risky but not uncertain, or in an environment that is uncertain. The decision rules are depicted in table 1.

Table 1

Expected Utility Decision Rules

Actor's Risk Orientation	Environmental Constraint	
	Risk	**Uncertainty**
Risk Acceptant	$E(U_i) = E(U_i)_b + \sum_{\ell=1}^{5} E(U_i)_{k_\ell}$	$E(U_i) = E(U_i)_b + \sum_{\ell=1}^{2} E(U_i)_{k_\ell}$
	if $E(U_i) \geq 0$, then i can, but need not, initiate a conflict with j.	if $E(U_i) \geq 0$, then i can, but need not, initiate a conflict with j.
	if $E(U_i) < 0$, then i cannot rationally initiate a conflict with j.	if $E(U_i) < 0$, then i cannot rationally initiate a conflict with j.
Risk Averse	$E(U_i) = E(U_i)_b + \sum_{\ell=1}^{5} E(U_i)_{k_\ell}$	$E(U_i) = E(U_i)_b + \Sigma E(U_i)_{k_\ell}$ given that only those third parties for whom $U_{iki} < U_{ikj}$ are entered into the calculation so that, $E(U_i)_{k_\ell} < 0$ by definition.
	if $E(U_i) \geq 0$ and $E(U_i)_b \geq 0$, then i can, but need not, initiate a conflict with j.	if $E(U_i) \geq 0$, then i can, but need not, initiate a conflict with j.
	if $E(U_i) < 0$ or $E(U_i) \geq 0$ but $E(U_i)_b < 0$, i cannot rationally initiate a conflict with j.	if $E(U_i) < 0$, given that it is defined to exclude third parties where $U_{iki} \geq U_{ikj}$, then i cannot rationally initiate a conflict with j.

51

Since both i and j are assumed to be rational expected utility maximizers, each is assumed to calculate its expected value in the event of a conflict. Without regard for whether i or j is the initiator—an issue that is not relevant to this discussion of decisions to escalate or resist escalation of a conflict—we can say that it is possible for the four mutually exclusive and exhaustive conditions depicted in figure 1 to arise. These four conditions are:

Condition 1:
Both Expect to Win

$$E(U_i) \geq 0 \quad \wedge \quad E(U_j) \geq 0$$

Condition 2:
One Expects to Win,
the Other Resists

$$E(U_i) \geq 0 \quad \wedge \quad E(U_j) < 0 \quad \wedge \quad |E(U_i)| \geq |E(U_j)| \quad \text{or}$$
$$E(U_j) \geq 0 \quad \wedge \quad E(U_i) < 0 \quad \wedge \quad |E(U_j)| \geq |E(U_i)|$$

Condition 3:
One Expects to Win,
the Other Yields

$$E(U_i) \geq 0 \quad \wedge \quad E(U_j) < 0 \quad \wedge \quad |E(U_i)| < |E(U_j)| \quad \text{or}$$
$$E(U_j) \geq 0 \quad \wedge \quad E(U_i) < 0 \quad \wedge \quad |E(U_j)| < |E(U_i)|$$

Condition 4:
Both Expect to Lose

$$E(U_i) < 0 \quad \wedge \quad E(U_j) < 0$$

The first condition (hereafter called "WIN") defines the circumstance under which both parties to a conflict expect to win. Since each side expects a net gain from the conflict, each nation's leaders have a strong incentive to resist the demands made by their adversaries. As neither i nor j has much incentive to fulfill demands or to negotiate them, escalation of hostilities is very likely under condition 1. Consequently, I expect rational leaders confronted with the circumstances of condition 1 to find that their conflicts tend to escalate to the level of war far more often than conflicts originating under other conditions.

Condition 2, which falls in the upper "bow tie" of figure 1, identifies situations in which only one party to a conflict expects to win, but in which the second party still has an incentive to resist the putative winner's demands. The incentive to resist (hereafter called "RESIST") arises because the expected winner is demanding more or larger benefits from the conflict than the expected loser anticipates losing. In these situations, we should not expect the anticipated loser to concede easily the demands made by the anticipated winner. Rather, we should expect that the putative loser will attempt to negotiate a compromise settlement which gives its opponent less than the opponent demanded at the outset. Should those negotiations fail—which is reasonably likely,

Figure 1

Conditions Influencing Conflict Escalation

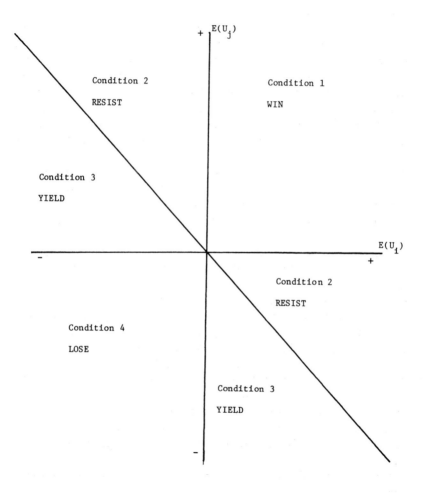

given that the nation with positive expected utility believes it can obtain the gains it is demanding—the conflict is likely to escalate to the level of war. Thus, in this situation, conflicts should be expected to have considerable variation in their tendency to escalate, with some being settled through negotiations without escalation, some being settled after moderate escalation, and still others being settled only after war.

Under the third condition (hereafter called "YIELD"), the nation with positive expected utility makes demands that are modest in comparison to the magnitude of losses that the other nation believes it is likely to incur in a war. The nation with negative expected utility, therefore, has no incentive to resist the demands of its adversary. Rather, the expected loser has incentives to concede to the demands of its adversary. The anticipated loser perceives the concessions demanded of it to be less than those the adversary could have extracted through the use of force. Under the YIELD condition, however, there is a possibility that the nation with positive expected utility, having had its demands fulfilled, finds its appetite whetted for larger concessions. In such cases, actors with positive expected utility might increase their demands sufficiently to prompt resistance from the adversary, creating a circumstance under which their conflict might escalate into a violent confrontation.

When the fourth condition arises (hereafter called "LOSE"), both nations expect to lose. According to the theory, this means that the leader who initiated the conflict by making a demand must be bluffing when s/he threatens reprisals if the demand is not fulfilled. This follows because we never anticipate a utility maximizer with negative expected utility to start a war. Presumably, the initiator hopes to gain some benefit by bluffing that s/he does not believe s/he can take by force. The adversary, also having negative expected utility for war, similarly does not expect to benefit from resisting. If the adversary chooses to bluff resistance, it is very unlikely that the first actor will risk escalating the conflict to secure benefits it does not believe it can gain. If the second adversary does not bluff resistance, no basis exists for escalation. Thus, under the LOSE condition, conflicts are not expected to produce resistance, escalation, or war.

The preceding discussion can be summarized with the following hypotheses:

H1: The probability of war is highest under the WIN condition;

H2: The probability of war under the RESIST condition—when one nation has positive expected utility and the other has an incentive to resist the demands of the first—is higher than under the YIELD or LOSE conditions;

54

H3: The probability of war under the YIELD condition is higher than under the LOSE condition, but is lower than under conditions 1 or 2;

H4: The probability of war under the LOSE condition is equal to zero.

The hypotheses are tested by analyzing a set of 251 international conflicts identified by Gochman (1975) and Singer and Small (1972), and updated by Bueno de Mesquita (1981). The conflicts are divided into three levels of hostility: threats, interventions, and wars. Gochman defines inter-state interventions as "hostilities between armed forces involving at least one member state of the inter-state system on each side, or hostilities between the armed forces of a member state directed against the territory and people of another member state" (Gochman, 1975: A-5). He defines an inter-state threat as an "explicit verbal statement by a high official on behalf of a member state's government declaring an intent to use military force against another member state for other than strictly defensive purposes; or, overt mobilization of armed forces by a member state, during periods of dispute or high tension, clearly directed against another member state for other than strictly defensive purposes." Gochman's data on threats and interventions include only those events in which at least one participant was a major power. Research is currently underway to extend my analysis to a recently completed compilation of threats and interventions that did not include major powers. Wars are defined here in accordance with the rules delineated in Singer and Small (1972). For purposes of this study, I assume that all conflicts—whether they involve threats, interventions, or war—begin with some demand. Escalation is then defined as the level of hostility that the conflict attains in response to the demand. A conflict that was coded as a threat is treated as having had the lowest level of hostility. Conflicts that involve interventions are treated as having escalated to an intermediate level of hostility. Wars, of course, are identified as those conflicts that have escalated to the highest level of hostility.

The independent variables are constructed from the expected utility scores reported in Bueno de Mesquita (1981). The utility terms in the equations summarized earlier are measured by using as a proxy the correlations between one nation's array of formal military alliance agreements and the other actor's array of formal military alliances.

Kendall's tau b is the correlation coefficient used to assess the congruence between alliance arrays, with alliance agreements ranked ordinally from most sacrifice of decision-maker autonomy to least sacrifice of decision-maker autonomy. Defense pacts are assumed to represent the greatest sacrifice of autonomy, then nonagression or neutrality pacts, then ententes, and finally, no alliance agreement. The probability terms in the equations are measured using the composite capabilities scores (Singer, Bremer, and Stuckey 1972) developed by the Correlates of War project. The probability of success in a conflict for a particular nation is defined as the proportion of i and j's capabilities that nation i represents. When a third party is involved, its composite capabilities are added to the relevant others capabilities (to i's when the equation views the third party as supporting i, or to j's when the equation views the third party as supporting j), and also to the denominator following the procedures delineated in Bueno de Mesquita (1980, 1981).

To test the hypotheses, it is necessary to define what I mean by the probability of a threat, intervention, or war under each of the escalation conditions. I estimate the theoretical probability of each type of conflict by dividing the number of instances of each type of conflict under each of the conditions by the total number of times the given condition occurs. For example, both belligerents had positive expected utility for war in 19 cases of conflict. Of these, 13 became wars. Thus the probability of war given the WIN condition is equal to 13 ÷ 19, or .684. Table 2 states the observed proportion of conflicts of each type under each expected utility condition. These proportions are treated as probabilities.

To evaluate the first hypothesis, it is appropriate to calculate the probability of war, given the WIN condition, and compare it to the probability of war under each other condition. To conduct such a test, I compute a z-score based on the normal approximation to the Bernoulli distribution. In this test, the analyst is asked to compare the actual frequency of war to the expected frequency, given some a priori determination of the "probability of success" p (that is, war) and the "probability of failure" q (that is, no war). The a priori value for the probability of success—p—is simply equal to the proportion of RESIST, YIELD, and LOSE cases that become wars. Thus, I compare the proportion of cases having become wars under the WIN condition to the proportion under all other conditions, with a positive z-score indicating that the frequency of war under the WIN condition is larger than expected, given the a priori probability of war under all other conditions. A negative z-score would, conversely, indicate that wars are less likely than expected under the WIN condition.

Table 2

The Probability of Each Conflict Type

Under Each Theoretical Condition

Condition	N	Probability of War	Probability of Intervention	Probability of Threat
WIN	19	.684 (13)*	.263 (5)	.053 (1)
RESIST	132	.394 (52)	.341 (45)	.265 (35)
YIELD	83	.133 (11)	.530 (44)	.337 (28)
LOSE	17	.000 (0)	.471 (8)	.529 (9)

Chi Squared = 39.447 (6 degrees of freedom) p < .01

*Numbers in parentheses represent the number of conflicts in the relevant category.

In the first test of hypotheses 1, $p = .272$ and $q = .728$. That is, 63 of 232 conflicts under conditions 2 through 4 became wars, or 27.2 percent. The calculation of $z = (X - Np)/\sqrt{Npq}$, where X in this case is the number of wars that occurred under the WIN condition, while N is the total number of cases in which both sides expected to win. Thus, X is 13 and N is 19 in this case. The z-score for this first test of the first hypothesis is 4.038, which is, of course, statistically significant at less than the .01 level.

A second, and more stringent, test of the first hypothesis is to determine whether the probability of war under condition 1 is significantly greater than the probability of war under the adjacent category (RESIST). In this case, $p = .394$ and $q = .606$, with $z = 2.589$. This score is also significant at less than the .01 level. The first hypothesis seems to be strongly supported by the evidence.

Each of the remaining hypotheses can be tested using the same technique applied to the first hypothesis. Doing so, I find that the probability of war, given the RESIST condition (.394), is significantly higher than under the subsequent conditions ($p = .111$, $q = .889$), with $z = 10.348$. Retesting this hypothesis against only the adjacent condition (YIELD) produces a z-score of 8.829. Both of these results are significant at much less than the .01 level. Turning to the third hypothesis, the evidence indicates that the probability of war under condition 3 is, as expected, higher than the probability of war under condition 4 (LOSE). Under the latter expected utility condition, no crisis in my data set became a war. This is, of course, precisely the war frequency anticipated in the fourth hypothesis. In other words, all four hypotheses are strongly supported by the evidence, with each mutually exclusive condition establishing a significantly different probability of war than the other, and with those probabilities declining sharply as the incentive to resist demands declines.

CONCLUSIONS

Three inferences may be drawn from this research. An important objective in any scientific enterprise is to achieve cumulative results. Only by linking dependent variables together within a common, rigorous, and explicit theoretical framework can we hope to piece together the international conflict puzzle (Zinnes, 1980). This study takes one step in that direction. The dependent variable investigated here—the level of conflict—is explained using results derived from an expected utility theory that has already shown some ability to account for conflict initiation, conflict intensity, and conflict expansion beyond two parties. The analysis reported here in conjunction with the other applications of this expected utility theory suggest some movement toward solving part of the conflict puzzle.

A second inference is that—despite the argument that leaders lose control once conflict is underway, so that events propel themselves forward in response to the ebb and flow of conflict—the evidence supports the notion that conflict escalation decisions are made as if by rational, expected utility maximizing leaders. Third, since we can know the relationship between expected utility values before a conflict is actually underway, we can improve our estimation of the likelihood of a threat, intervention, or war over that which is possible simply by examining the expected utility score of a potential initiator. Indeed, with suitable refinement of the theoretical form and the operational procedures, there is reason to believe that the expected utility framework can help forecast conflict and, ultimately, manipulate its probability.

REFERENCES

Altfeld, M., and Bueno de Mesquita, B. 1979. Choosing Sides in Wars. *International Studies Quarterly* March:87-112.

Berkowitz, B. 1981. *A Theory of Realignment.* Paper prepared for delivery at the 1981 annual meeting of the American Political Science Association.

Bueno de Mesquita, B. 1981. *The War Trap.* New Haven: Yale University Press.

_____. 1980. An Expected Utility Theory of International Conflict. *American Political Science Review* December:917-31.

Gochman, C. 1975. *Status, Conflict, and War: The Major Powers,* 1820-1970. Ph.D. Dissertation, University of Michigan.

Singer, J. D.; Bremer, S.; and Stuckey, J. 1972. Capability Distribution, Uncertainty, and Major Power War, 1820-1965. In *Peace, War, and Numbers,* ed. B. Russett. Beverly Hills, CA: Sage.

Singer, J. D., and Small, M. 1972. *The Wages of War.* New York: John Wiley & Sons.

Zinnes, D. 1980. Three Puzzles in Search of a Researcher: Presidential Address. *International Studies Quarterly* September:315-42.

3

ALLIANCE BEHAVIOR AND THE APPROACH TO WORLD WAR I: THE USE OF BIVARIATE NEGATIVE BINOMIAL DISTRIBUTIONS

Manus I. Midlarsky

One of the most important periods in contemporary international history is the approximate half century leading to the onset of World War I. In some respects, this time span is a conundrum. The nineteenth century was, for the most part, a time of relatively peaceful relations among the European powers. The European comity of nations was seen as having reached a zenith of cultural and scientific achievement; indeed, the concept of a European civilization was widespread (Pradt, 1800; Vattel, 1870). Nevertheless, a war of catastrophic dimension erupted, the consequences of which, of course, we are still experiencing. Thus, we have numerous studies of the nineteenth century itself as a time of relative tranquility (e.g., Gulick, 1955), and then, in stark contrast, studies of that time span in the late nineteenth and early twentieth centuries when the escalation leading to the violence took place. (Cf. the contrast by one author alone—Langer, 1929 and 1966—in which the immediate post-1871 period is treated in virtually complete isolation from the period beginning with the Franco-Russian alliance.)

Here, in the approach to World War I, we have an illustration of systemic breakdown. From a relatively harmonious set of European relationships in the early to mid-nineteenth century, the entire system rapidly began to collapse toward the end of the century, around the time of the Franco-Russian alliance. This may, in fact, illustrate Cioffi's conceptualization of political reliability, wherein a breakdown of each individual component (e.g., England's long-held neutrality in

This study was supported by a grant of the National Science Foundation, SES 80-25047.

61

continental affairs) can have a disproportionate impact on the political evolution of the system. In the following analysis, the overall development of the system will be studied over a relatively long time period in order to examine its trajectory as it approaches the onset of World War I.

The events subsequent to the Franco-Russian alliance, such as the Anglo-French understanding of 1904, the Bosnian crisis of 1908 and the Balkan Wars, are seen as the progenitors of World War I. Seldom is a time span selected prior to World War I long enough to consider the changes which took place over time. Here, such a study is undertaken in order to reveal such changes, where they occurred, and specifically with respect to alliance behavior as both a major international process and an indicator of change in international structure. The time period of concern is 1871-1914, a 44-year span which begins with the formation of the German Empire and ends with the onset of World War I. A new international structure and attendant set of relations now has been formed in the heart of Europe, so the consequences of these events can be traced until 1914. No alliance relationships existing prior to 1871 survived beyond that year so that a *tabula rasa* with regard to alliance formation exists at that time.

A related question concerns the transformation of fundamental processes toward the end of the nineteenth century. A major invariant during most of that century was the maintenance of an alliance equilibrium. In an era when citizen armies were largely absent and the weapons technology was mostly unchanging (except toward the end of the century), alliances were the principal means by which power shifts were effected (Holsti, 1976). The prevailing balance of power of that period tended to be identified with the maintenance of a power equilibrium (Zinnes, 1967), the dominant characteristics of which could be seriously affected only by changes in alliance formation.

A hypothetical alliance equilibrium equation was established (Midlarsky, 1981) wherein the probability of i alliances being created, C_i, was, on the average, set equal to the probability of i dissolutions, D_i, within some time interval, t, or

$$C_i = <D_i>_{AV} = \sum_{n=i}^{\infty} P(n)D_i \qquad (1)$$

where $P(n)$ is the probability that n alliances exist during t. In this fashion, if an alliance partner is lost at some point in time, then that power loss will be regained at some future time as the result of a new alliance formation. A mathematical consequence of equation (1) is the

Poisson expression for alliance formation, C_i, which was found to hold true for the nineteenth century by McGowan and Rood (1975). Equations for transition probabilities for the number of alliances existing from one year to the next were further derived from equation (1) and these equations were found to be mostly obeyed in the nineteenth century. What then characterizes the changes in international process toward the end of the nineteenth century, which likely led to substantial departures from this equilibrium process?

Aside from the substantive problem of examining changes in international process and structure prior to a major conflict, there exists an important methodological problem—the troublesome and still-nagging question of distinguishing adequately among the various sources of interdependence in probabilistic analyses—which is now potentially resolvable. There exists now a relatively long history of the use of "contagious" distributions such as the negative binomial in the analysis of various kinds of interdependent political behavior ranging from Latin American military coups (Midlarsky, 1970) to wars (Davis, Duncan and Siverson, 1978), terrorism (Midlarsky, et al., 1980), and perhaps most importantly, alliances (Job, 1976; Siverson and Duncan, 1976; Midlarsky, 1981).[1]

In all of these studies, the principal distribution used was the negative binomial which incorporates the assumption of different propensities on the part of the units (e.g., countries) toward experiencing the phenomenon in question, in contrast to, for example, the Poisson which is based on an assumption of homogeneity. The difficulty is that it is virtually impossible to differentiate between heterogeneity as an *inherently* different propensity to experience the events in question, diffusion as an increased probability after another unit has experienced such an event, or reinforcement as an increased probability for the unit after its own past experience includes instances of this behavior. The univariate distributions themselves will not yield such differentiations without added information.

Bivariate distributions, however, hold promise for incorporating such differentiations. Precisely because they can be tailored to examine changes over time, bivariate probability distributions could potentially reveal differences between, for example, diffusion on the one hand, and inherently different propensities as in heterogeneity on the other. Two such bivariate distributions, in fact, will now be explored in an analysis of alliance behavior leading to World War I. The first distribution is a compound Poisson distribution incorporating the assumption of different propensities as in varying policy preferences for alliance formation. This is the heterogeneity hypothesis. The second is a distribution incorporating the assumption of diffusion wherein the propensities toward experiencing the phenomenon increase after the first event. Strictly speaking, as will be seen, this is a reinforcement distribution, but, under certain conditions, the inference of diffusion is clearly made.

HETEROGENEITY AND DIFFUSION

The compound Poisson distribution is derived under the assumption that there exists a mixture of homogeneous populations each with its own proportion and expectation μ, such that if there are two such central tendencies (Arbous and Kerrich, 1951:401), then,

$$p(x) = p_1(\mu_1)e^{-\mu_1} \frac{(\mu_1)^x}{x!} + p_2(\mu_2)e^{-\mu_2} \frac{(\mu_2)^x}{x!} \text{ where } p_1 + p_2 = 1.$$

More generally, we can say that

$$p(x) = \sum_{i=1}^{k} p_i(\mu_i)e^{-\mu_i}\frac{(\mu_i)^x}{x!} \text{ where } \Sigma p_i = 1.$$

This is the defining assumption of the compound Poisson formulation and leads directly to the negative binomial distribution in the form (Arbous and Kerrich, 1951:403)

$$p(x) = (\frac{r}{m+r})^r \frac{\Gamma(x+r)}{x!\Gamma(r)} (\frac{m}{m+r})^x \tag{2}$$

where Γ is the gamma function, m and σ^2 are the mean and variance, respectively, of the observed distribution and

$$r = \frac{m^2}{\sigma^2-m}. \tag{3}$$

A somewhat more easily recognized version is seen in Derman, et al. (1973:283)

$$p(x) = \binom{x + r - 1}{r-1} q^r (1-q)^x \tag{4}$$

where r is defined as above and

$$q = \frac{m}{\sigma^2}. \tag{5}$$

The translation of equation (2) into equation (4) is effected by setting q = r/m + r and $\Gamma(r) = (r-1)!$ when r is a positive integer.

A bivariate compound distribution is obtained when the variable x is divided into two parts wherein

$$x = x_0 + x_1$$

and x_0 is the number of alliances a country experiences during the interval δ_0, x_1 is the number of alliances during δ_1, and $\delta = \delta_0 + \delta_1$, where δ is the overall time period during which x alliances are entered into.

Assume now that each country has a constant probability μ across both portions δ_0 and δ_1 of the time interval and that for each individual

$$p(x_0/\mu) = e^{-\mu\delta_0} \frac{(\mu\delta_0)^{x_0}}{x_0!} \text{ and } p(x_1/\mu) = e^{-\mu\delta_1} \frac{(\mu\delta_1)^{x_1}}{x_1!}.$$

The parameter μ here is a fixed annual alliance rate unaffected by time, but different for each country. Under these assumptions x_0, x_1 and x all have negative binomial distributions and the joint bivariate compound Poisson distribution is given by (Arbous and Kerrich, 1951:415)

$$P(x_0, x_1) = \frac{r^r \alpha^x}{(r + \alpha\delta)^{r+x}} \frac{\Gamma(r+x)}{\Gamma(r)} \frac{\delta_0^{x_0} \delta_1^{x_1}}{x_0! x_1!} \quad (6)$$

with

$$\alpha = \frac{m}{\delta} \quad (7)$$

and

$$r = \frac{m^2}{\sigma^2 - m}. \quad (8)$$

Now under a different set of assumptions, we can derive an expression for the diffusion distribution. At time $t = 0$, none of the countries has experienced an alliance and each individual country has the same probability of entering into an alliance as any other. Later, however, the individual countries separate out—some have had no alliances, others have had one, two, or more. Each country then can have a varying probability of forming an alliance depending on its earlier experience. Those having had an alliance are more likely to have another than those that did not. In practice, as we shall see, it is impossible to tell simply from the distribution if the imitation is self-reinforcing as in a reinforcement condition, or is other-reinforcing as in a diffusion effect.

This assumption can be stated as

$$f(x,t) = \beta + \lambda x \tag{9}$$

where x, as before, is the number of alliances in existence, β and λ are constants, and f(x,t) is a time-varying propensity to experience alliances. In this instance, equation (9) states that the propensity increases linearly with each added alliance by a country. With these assumptions, one arrives at the distribution (Arbous and Kerrich, 1951:411)

$$p(x,t) = e^{-\beta t}\, \frac{\Gamma(\beta/\lambda + x)}{x!(\beta/\lambda)}\, (1\text{-}e^{-\lambda t})^x \tag{10}$$

which is a negative binomial distribution of the same form as equation (2) with $(1\text{-}e^{-\lambda t})$ in place of $m/m+r$, and replaced by β/λ.

This univariate distribution then will give exactly the same results as equation (2), albeit with the inherently different assumption of equation (9). The bivariate version of equation (10) will, however, yield differential results from its counterpart, equation (6). This distribution is given by (Arbous and Kerrich, 1951:421)

$$P(x_0,x_1) = e^{-\beta\delta}\, \frac{\Gamma(\beta/\lambda) + x)}{\Gamma(\beta/\lambda)x_0!x_1!}\, (e^{-\lambda\delta_1} - e^{-\lambda\delta})^{x_0}\, (1 - e^{-\lambda\delta_1})^{x_1} \tag{11}$$

where x, x_0, x_1, δ, δ_0, δ_1 are defined exactly as before and

$$e^{\delta\lambda} = \frac{\sigma^2}{m} \tag{12}$$

and

$$\beta = \frac{m\lambda}{e^{\delta\lambda}-1}. \tag{13}$$

These are the distributions (equations [6] and [11]) to be compared empirically. Note that equation (6) is symmetric in that, given equal length subintervals δ_0 and δ_1, then $P(x_0, x_1)$ is equal to $P(x_1, x_0)$. This is not true for equation (11) because of the time-varying nature of f(x, t) which is reflected by higher values of $P(x_1, x_3)$, for example, in comparison with $P(x_3, x_1)$.

66

DATA AND ANALYSIS

The data to be analyzed here are those of the Correlates of War Project (COW) (Singer and Small, 1966; Small and Singer, 1969) and include all alliances involving major European powers (Austria-Hungary, Germany, Russia, France and Great Britain) between 1871 and 1914. Alliances exclusively between minor powers are omitted.

Only the nations that were part of the European system are included. The defining criterion was that the country either was geographically situated on the continent of Europe or experienced alliance or war with European powers. The war must have occurred on the continent of Europe or must have involved European powers on the territory of some non-European country. Further, to be included, all countries must have become independent prior to the midpoint of the time span, here 1892. Because Norway (1905) and Bulgaria (1908) violated the independence requirement, and the United States violated the war location requirement, they were not included.[2]

Note that the basic assumption of no alliances existing at $t = 0$ is met. The COW list treats all prior alliances as having terminated at the end of the Franco-Prussian War in 1871. As suggested here and in prior research (Job, 1976; Siverson and Duncan, 1976; Midlarsky, 1981), the univariate distribution shown in table 1 is negative binomial using equations (3) and (5) for the estimation of parameters. Of course, one cannot distinguish among the various possible sources of fit for this distribution alone. We must turn now to the bivariate distributions given in equations (6) and (11).

Table 2 presents the observed bivariate distribution over the two equal and nonoverlapping time intervals of 1871-1892 and 1893-1914. All alliances formed in the earlier interval, of course, were counted for that interval. In addition, alliances that continued to exist beyond the midpoint of the second interval (1903) also were counted for the second. In practice, virtually all of the alliances which terminated after 1903 actually continued until 1914 so that there was little doubt in the counting operation. These observed values can be seen in table 2. The observed bivariate distribution in the table is the one to be differentially modeled by equations (6) and (11).

Table 1

Observed and Predicted Values of the Negative Binomial
Distribution for Alliances in Existence, 1871-1914

Number of Alliances, n	Observed Number of Countries with n Alliances Existing	Predicted Number of Countries with n Alliances Existing $q = .2282$ $r = .9961$
0	6	4.36
1	4	3.35
2	1	2.58
3	1	1.99
4	1	1.53
5	0 ⎤	1.18[a] ⎤
6	1	.91
7	2	.70
8	1	.54
9	0 ⎬ 6	.42 ⎬ 5.19
10	0	.32
11	1	.25
12	1	.19
>12	0 ⎦	.68 ⎦

$\chi^2 = 2.513$, df = 3, p < .50

[a]This category and all below it are combined for the chi-square test.

Table 2

Observed Bivariate Distribution of the Number of Countries
with n Number of Alliances in Existence, 1871-1914

	n	1893-1914									Total
		0	1	2	3	4	5	6	7	8	
	0	6	2	0	0	1	0	0	0	0	9
	1	2	1	1	0	0	1	0	0	0	5
	2	0	0	0	0	0	1	0	0	0	1
1871-1892	3	0	0	0	0	0	0	0	0	0	0
	4	0	0	0	0	1	0	0	0	0	1
	5	0	0	1	0	0	0	0	1	0	2
	6	0	0	0	0	0	0	0	0	0	0
	7	0	0	0	0	0	0	0	0	0	0
	8	0	0	0	1	0	0	0	0	0	1
Total		8	3	2	1	2	2	0	1	0	19

68

Table 3

Predicted Bivariate Distribution of the Number of Countries
With n Number of Alliances by the Compound Poisson Distribution
(α = .07656, r = .99611)

| | | 1893–1914 | | | | | | | | |
n	0	1	2	3	4	5	6	7	8	Total
0	4.36	1.68	.65	.25	.10	.04	.01	.01	.00	7.10
1	1.68	1.30	.75	.39	.19	.09	.04	.02	.01	4.47
2	.65	.75	.58	.39	.22	.13	.06	.03	.01	2.82
3	.25	.39	.39	.29	.22	.12	.07	.04	.02	1.79
4	.10	.19	.22	.22	.15	.10	.07	.04	.02	1.11
5	.04	.09	.13	.12	.10	.08	.06	.04	.02	.68
6	.01	.04	.06	.07	.07	.06	.04	.03	.02	.40
7	.01	.02	.03	.04	.04	.04	.03	.03	.02	.26
8	.00	.01	.01	.02	.02	.02	.02	.02	.01	.13
Total	7.10	4.47	2.82	1.79	1.11	.68	.40	.26	.13	18.76

(left margin label: 1871–1892)

Table 4

Predicted Bivariate Distribution of the Number of Countries
With n Number of Alliances by the Diffusion Distribution
(β = .03345, λ = .03358)

| | | 1893–1914 | | | | | | | | |
n	0	1	2	3	4	5	6	7	8	Total
0	4.36	2.27	1.18	.62	.32	.17	.09	.05	.02	9.08
1	1.09	1.13	.88	.62	.40	.25	.15	.09	.05	4.66
2	.27	.42	.44	.38	.30	.22	.15	.10	.07	2.35
3	.07	.14	.18	.19	.17	.15	.11	.09	.06	1.16
4	.02	.04	.07	.08	.09	.08	.07	.06	.05	.56
5	.00	.01	.02	.03	.04	.04	.04	.03	.03	.24
6	.00	.00	.01	.01	.02	.02	.02	.02	.02	.12
7	.00	.00	.00	.00	.00	.01	.01	.01	.01	.04
8	.00	.00	.00	.00	.00	.00	.00	.00	.00	.00
Total	5.81	4.01	2.78	1.93	1.34	.94	.64	.45	.31	18.21

(left margin label: 1871–1892)

69

Table 3 shows the results of this effort using the compound Poisson assumption of equation (6), with the estimation of parameters by equations (7) and (8). Table 4 demonstrates the consequences of testing the diffusion assumption of equation (11), using equations (12) and (13) for the estimation of parameters. Because of the large number of 0 values, necessitated by the small n and lengthy time period, the row and column totals are analyzed separately. This also allows for the possibility of differential outcomes wherein each of the models is not wholly applicable or inapplicable, but applies to one time period and not to the other. This, of course, could not be assessed directly from the bivariate entries themselves.

The comparisons of goodness of fit are found in table 5. The distribution (11) incorporating the diffusion assumption does give a better fit for both time periods. This is especially true for predicting the tail of the distribution in 1893-1914. This model does a far better job of predicting the tail of the distribution than does the compound Poisson, although some error is incurred in the lower values of n in the distribution. This disparity in prediction between the two segments will be treated shortly.

Table 5

Comparisons of the Goodness of Fit of the Compound Poisson and Diffusion Distributions

	1871-1892			1893-1914		
n	Observed	Compound	Diffusion	Observed	Compound	Diffusion
0	9	7.10	9.08	8	7.10	5.81
1	5	4.47	4.66	3	4.47	4.01
2	1	2.82	2.35	2	2.82	2.78
3	0	1.79	1.16⌝[a]	1	1.79	1.93
4	1⌝[a]	1.11⌝[a]	.56	2⌝	1.11⌝	1.34⌝
5	2	.68	.24	2	.68	.94
6	0 ⎱ 4	.40 ⎱ 2.82	.12 ⎱ 2.92	0 ⎱ 5	.40 ⎱ 2.82	.64 ⎱ 4.47
7	0	.26	.04	1	.26	.45
8	1	.13	.01	0	.13	.31
>8	0⌟	.24⌟	.79⌟	0⌟	.24⌟	.79⌟

$$\chi^2 = 4.030, \text{ df} = 2 \qquad \chi^2 = 1.201, \text{ df} = 1 \qquad \chi^2 = 2.870, \text{ df} = 2 \qquad \chi^2 = 1.810, \text{ df} = 2$$
$$p < .20 \qquad\qquad p < .30 \qquad\qquad p < .30 \qquad\qquad p < .50$$

[a]This category and those below it are combined for the chi-square tests.

Although the overall fit of the diffusion model is superior even for the earlier 1871-1892 interval, certain additional features of this alliance behavior still may be examined. If, in the third column of table 5, the value of 1.16 were not combined with the remaining values in order to achieve a minimum value of 1.5 (as suggested by Gibbons [1971:72]), then the overall chi-square statistic would be equal to 4.812, df = 2; it would actually be slightly larger, with the same number of degrees of freedom, than that for the compound Poisson or heterogeneity distribution. Thus, an inference of some heterogeneity could be made for the 1871-1892 time interval. This calculation illustrates not only the sensitivity of the chi-square analysis to small values, and hence the extreme caution which should be used in maintaining them as separate categories, but also that some mixture of heterogeneity and diffusion could be operating in this earlier interval. Whatever its extent, however, this heterogeneity would be confined to the tail of the distribution where the great powers are found in their high level of alliance activity.

Consider the lower values of n of the observed distribution for 1871-1892 in table 5. They are reasonably well predicted by the distribution (11) incorporating diffusion, but then this distribution does not do quite as well for the tail portion. Recall that an assumption of the derivation of the distribution was that initially there should be a random propensity for alliance formation; but this propensity changes over time, in a differential manner, for the various countries comprising the set. Thus, there should be a tendency towards Poisson alliance behavior at the outset, and the third column of table 5 suggests that this randomness is confined to the upper rows of the distribution where the small number of alliances per country do not yet reflect the differential propensities of the various countries towards alliance formation.

The test of randomness for the first four rows is found in table 6. The fit is a good one as measured by the chi-square statistic. With this hypothesis of randomness confirmed, it can now be seen that whatever heterogeneity is contained in that distribution is due to those countries found in rows 4-8. Thus, the heterogeneity which exists is not uniform in the sense of varying propensities across all of the participants, but rather one confined to the countries in the tail of the distribution—Austria-Hungary, Germany, Russia and Italy.

At the same time, it is clear that the distribution (11) incorporating diffusion does not predict the upper portion of the 1893-1914 distribution very well, despite being the best fit among the alternatives. It is to this somewhat anomalous outcome that we now turn.

Table 6

Observed and Poisson Predicted Values of the Number of Alliances
in Existence for the Truncated Distribution, 1871-1892

Number of Alliances, n	Observed Number of Countries with n Alliances Existing	Predicted Number of Countries with n Alliances Existing u = .4667
0	9	9.41
1	5	4.39
2	1	1.02[a]
3	0	.16

$$\chi^2 = .130, \text{ df} = 1, p < .80$$

[a]The bottom two categories are combined for the chi-square test.

72

BOSE-EINSTEIN STATISTICS
AND THE GEOMETRIC DISTRIBUTION

A hallmark of a diffusion process is indistinguishability. From a condition of the rather infrequent and therefore scarce alliance formation at the start of the 1871-1892 period, all of the great powers are involved in the alliance process. Even France, initially remote if not excluded from the alliance process of the nineteenth century, became involved via the Franco-Russian alliance; England, which had remained entirely aloof from continental alliances, eventually succumbed in the form of the 1904 and 1907 understandings, respectively, with France and Russia.

The question, then, is whether there is a distribution which can model the eventual indistinguishability (in regard to alliance formation) of the various powers. There does, in fact, exist a distribution which incorporates the assumption of indistinguishability of the units. It is known as the basis for Bose-Einstein statistics (Feller, 1968:61; Ijiri and Simon, 1977:83-93). If we consider various countries as dots, and the alliances among them as compartments between the dots, then the assumption of indistinguishability of the dots can be modeled as follows. At first, there are very few compartments corresponding to an infrequent and selective alliance formation, but when more of these compartments appear at random dividing the nations, then effectively there is no difference between countries with regard to alliance formation. This is shown in the following diagram in an arrangement of dots (countries) among compartments (alliances). (For extended versions of this derivation, see ter Haar, 1954:74-75, and Mayer and Mayer, 1940:438.)

If there are C compartments and N dots to be distributed among the compartments, then the first compartment can be chosen in any one of C ways. Once having chosen this particular compartment, the boundary of this compartment may have one of the remaining C-1 compartments on its right, or one of the N dots. The total number of ways in which these N dots and C-1 compartments can be arranged is N + C-1; together with the C ways of selecting the first compartment, this gives $\{(C-1)+N\}!$ ways of arranging the N dots among the C compartments. However, the dots are indistinguishable, and as a result, any arrangements among the dots or among the compartments themselves must be eliminated. These are, respectively, N! and C! and so our expression W, for the number of ways N dots can be distributed among C compartments, is

$$W = \frac{C \, \{(C\text{-}1) + N\}!}{C! \, N!}.$$

$$= \frac{\{(C\text{-}1) + N\}!}{(C\text{-}1)! \, N!}. \tag{14}$$

In the limiting case of N and C approaching infinity, the ratio N/C approaches a mean μ, and the limiting distribution for the probability that a given compartment contains j dots, W_j, is given by (Feller, 1968:61; Tolman, 1962:512):

$$W_j = \frac{\mu^j}{(\mu+1)} j+1 \qquad j = 0, 1, 2, \ldots \tag{15}$$

where j is some integer and W_j is a geometric distribution with variance

$$\sigma^2 = \mu^2 + \mu. \tag{16}$$

It is well known that the negative binomial distribution with $r = 1$ is a geometric distribution (Derman, et al., 1973:291); and indeed if r is set equal to one in equation (3), then

$$1 = \frac{\mu^2}{\sigma^2 \text{-} \mu}$$

or

$$\sigma^2 = \mu^2 + \mu$$

where μ is the mean of the distribution. This is precisely the same expression as in equation (16). If we now examine the value of r in table 1, we see that it is very close to 1. The predicted value of the variance by the right side of equation (16) is 14.7147 to be compared with the observed value of 14.7590. The error of prediction here is .3 percent.

Thus, the results demonstrate an excellent fit to the distribution resulting from the assumption of indistinguishability. Substantively, this means that by the end of the period there were no differences among any of the countries in regard to their propensity to ally. Thus, England was just as likely to ally as was France, Germany or Austria.

This stands in stark contrast to the behavior of England and France in the earlier portion of the period (1871-1892) in which these countries were highly differentiated in their alliance behavior from the remaining great powers.

The applicability of this univariate distribution also now suggests reasons for the much better fit of the predicted values for the tail of the observed distribution in the application of the negative binomial in table 1, and especially in the bivariate analysis of the period 1893-1914. The values in the tail are likely predicted better by the distribution incorporating diffusion because they include all of the great powers in the bottom rows of the table. The rows 0-3 contain many of the smaller powers; the category that is least well predicted (based on an absolute deviation from predication $|0_i-E_i|$ is the 0 row which includes countries such as Sweden or Denmark in the observed values. Clearly, these countries should not be accurately predicted in any distribution based on the assumption of indistinguishability with regard to alliance behavior, and they are not so predicted, based on the divergence between observed and predicted values. The single parameter geometric, then, not only provides a more parsimonious way of describing the data than does the negative binomial, but its derivation sheds light on the areas of best fit of the distribution (11) and those which are less good.

The issue of the correct process and also of nomenclature needs to be addressed, for we have been using the term *diffusion* as a generic description of alliance behavior during the 1893-1914 period. This is the only sensible interpretation of the results, for the alternative possibility of reinforcement is unlikely. The process of reinforcement implies that the prior experience of, for example, alliance formation leads to a higher probability of such behavior in the future. In the case of alliance behavior here, this simply would not be the case because we know from various historical accounts of the period (cf. Langer, 1929) that it was the reaction to the overall European, if not global, situation which inspired various countries such as England or France to ultimately join alliances—their prior alliance experience having virtually nothing to do with their later alliance formation. Further, countries such as Austria or Germany actually showed a decrease, with Russia and Italy remaining constant over the two halves of the overall time period, thus suggesting an absence of reinforcement in these instances. Contagion as a form of direct observation and unqualified imitation is ruled out because it is the character of alliance formation that each alliance is evaluated on its own merits and requires some sort of independent precipitating event. Additionally, contagion processes, in contrast to diffusion effects, have not been modeled successfully by probability distributions (Midlarsky, 1978).

The negative binomial as the appropriate model is derivable under the circumstances of independent initiations of events such as alliance formation but similar outcomes. The alliance as an international event clearly would be initiated by an independent event, such as a war between neighboring powers, but with the outcome of a protective alliance which is influenced by the behavior of previous alliances—more specifically, the countries forming those alliances—as in a diffusion condition. (An urn model for a diffusion process is developed in Midlarsky, et al., 1980:270-71.)

The question of learned behavior is important here. For countries such as England and France and smaller countries which earlier saw their security interests satisfied by means other than alliance formation (e.g., colonialism, strict neutrality), the diffusion of alliances in the 1893-1914 period represented a response similar to the behavior of other countries. Why a rapid diffusion of alliances occurred is a matter of some interest and will not be explored here in depth other than to suggest certain possibilities.

Apart from the structural aspect of rapidly shrinking colonial possibilities which turned Europe inward (Dehio, 1962) and the relative absence now of small powers (Midlarsky, 1981) which likely caused the larger powers to be more oriented to each other, the history of the period suggests that there was an inability to explore alternatives in an imaginative way. None of the diplomats of the later 1893-1914 period matched Bismarck in the ability to respond in a statesmanlike and balanced manner to the difficulties of European politics. Sir Edward Grey, the British Foreign Minister, was perhaps among the most able, but even he realized the folly of the European War in 1916 only after the death of his son in the war. (See Clive [1963] and especially Penson [1943] for the course of British foreign policy in this period.) Aerenthal, the Austrian Foreign Minister, was perhaps the most wily, if not the most competent of these, but he directed his attention almost exclusively (and perhaps rightly so, given his responsibilities) to the preservation of the Dual Monarchy by any and all means.

Prior to 1890, Bismarck had established an intricate and far-reaching series of alliances designed to keep the diplomatic advantage on the side of Germany but without serious risk of war. Now, with the departure of Bismarck, this same set of alliances in other hands, namely those of Wilhelm II, began to look more threatening than balancing. The response to threat, then, was more of the same alliance behavior (this time on the part of the future allies) which had, in the first instance, been designed to ensure peace. The end, of course, was war.

The fact that there was certainly no necessity for increased alliance formation, especially in the manner in which it occurred, adds further irony to this circumstance. (The concept of international risk-taking, both in relation to alignments and war, is developed in Bueno de Mesquita [1980].) Merritt and Clark (1977), for example, have shown that, based on mail flow data in the late nineteenth and early twentieth centuries, Russia should have been linked far more closely with the Triple Alliance countries, especially Germany, than to Britain or France. Concurrently, Italy, a member of the Triple Alliance until 1914, should have been linked with the Triple Entente, especially France, with whom she shared much economic activity. These alternative congruencies, based on communications linkages, do not necessarily suggest that alliances should have happened the way communications dictate. But rather, that alliances—insofar as they served a political purpose toward the end of the nineteenth century—were highly malleable devices, as Bismarck clearly saw. To have treated them in the almost inexorable manner of the early twentieth century was, in many respects, a violation of the spirit of their original intent.

CONCLUSION

This study has demonstrated the transformation of alliance behavior based on the diffusion of alliances subsequent to the Bismarckian period. A relatively stable system became transformed into an unstable one, perhaps through the intermediaries of several events, each of which may have contributed disproportionately to the ultimate systemic breakdown. Eventually, as we see in the Bose-Einstein geometric distribution analysis, the nations comprising the system became virtually indistinguishable with respect to alliance formation. Thus the instrument that may have been used for very different purposes at the outset of this period, became for all of the powers, a way of ensuring security, but with precisely the opposite consequences at the end.

Methodologically, now for the first time we can clearly distinguish between heterogeneity as inherently different policy orientations and diffusion. Although the expressions (6) and (11) cannot in themselves distinguish between reinforcement as a self-augmenting process and the diffusion effect, or imitation of others, that distinction often can be made from the context in which the behaviors occur. Further, the geometric distribution (15) can be used in certain instances as a single parameter distribution to model diffusion. Certainly it is more efficient than the negative binomial in that it requires only one parameter, the mean; in addition, it incorporates the assumption of indistinguishability which may be necessary for the diffusion effect to take hold. However, the units all should be sufficiently alike so that this model could not be used with very large samples or populations including many large and small powers. It is possible that the sample size here may already be the limit of what can be accomplished using this distribution. The requirements of a parsimonious model of this type may include the a priori elimination of major dissimilarities among the units in question.

NOTES

1. Mathematical statisticians such as Feller (1943), Greenwood and Yule (1928) or Arbous and Kerrich (1951) have used the term contagion either to refer to reinforcement processes, defined below, or to what is here called diffusion. In the present study, the three processes are differentiated, with contagion specifically reserved for the direct imitation by an observer of prototype behavior, not requiring any precipitant, in contrast to diffusion or reinforcement, as imitation which requires independent precipitants for the triggering of the behavior in question. The precipitant is independent of the behavior itself, but the consequences of the precipitating agent are dependent on past behavior (e.g., repressive acts by an authoritarian government leading to a terrorist response on the part of dissidents as a consequence of the prior use of terrorism elsewhere). Reinforcement is a self-augmenting process dependent on the unit's own past experience with the behavior, in contrast to diffusion which is dependent on the behavior of other units. For additional details, see Midlarsky (1978), Midlarsky, et al. (1980) and Most and Starr (1980).

2. The countries included are listed in the central system in Singer and Small (1968) and are: Austria-Hungary, Belgium, China, Denmark, England, France, Germany, Greece, Holland, Italy, Japan, Portugal, Romania, Russia, Serbia, Spain, Sweden, Switzerland, Turkey.

REFERENCES

Arbous, A. G., and Kerrich, J. E. 1951. Accident Statistics and the Concept of Accident Proneness. *Biometrics* 7:340-432.

Bueno de Mesquita, B. 1980. An Expected Utility Theory of International Conflict. *American Political Science Review* 74:917-31.

Clive, J. 1963. British History, 1870-1914, Reconsidered: Recent Trends in the Historiography of the Period. *American Historical Review* 68:987-1009.

Davis, W. W.; Duncan, G. T.; and Siverson, R. M. 1978. The Dynamics of Warfare: 1816-1965. *American Journal of Political Science* 22:772-92.

Dehio, Ludwig. 1962. *The Precarious Balance: Four Centuries of the European Power Struggle,* Trans. Charles Fullman. New York: Knopf.

Derman, C.; Gleser, L. J.; and Olkin, I. 1973. *A Guide to Probability Theory and Application.* New York: Holt, Rinehart and Winston.

Feller, W. 1943. On a General Class of "Contagious" Distributions. *Annals of Mathematical Statistics* 14:389-400.

_____. 1968. *An Introduction to Probability Theory and its Applications,* Vol. I, 3rd Ed. New York:Wiley.

Gibbons, J. D. 1971. *Nonparametric Statistical Inference.* New York: McGraw-Hill.

Greenwood, M., and Yule, G. U. 1920. An Inquiry into the Nature of Frequency Distributions Representative of Multiple Happenings with Particular Reference to the Occurrence of Multiple Attacks of Disease or of Repeated Accidents. *Journal of the Royal Statistical Society* 83:255-79.

Gulick, E. V. 1955. *Europe's Classical Balance of Power.* Ithaca, New York: Cornell Univ. Press.

Holsti, O. R. 1976. Alliance and Coalition Diplomacy. In *World Politics: An Introduction,* J. N. Rosenau, W. Thompson, and G. Boyd (eds.), New York: The Free Press, pp. 337-72.

Ijiri, Y., and Simon, H. A. 1977. *Skew Distributions and the Sizes of Business Firms.* Amsterdam: North-Holland.

Job, B. 1976. Membership in Inter-nation Alliances, 1815-1965: An Exploration Utilizing Mathematical Probability Models. In *Mathematical Models in International Relations,* D. A. Zinnes and J. V. Gillespie (eds.), New York: Praeger, pp. 74-109.

Langer, W. L. 1966. *European Alliances and Alignments: 1871-1890,* 2nd ed. New York: Knopf.

_____. 1929. *The Franco-Russian Alliance: 1890-1894.* Cambridge: Harvard Univ. Press.

Mayer, J. E., and Mayer, M. G. 1940. *Statistical Mechanics.* New York: Wiley.

McGowan, P. J., and Rood, R. M. 1975. Alliance Behavior in Balance of Power Systems: Applying a Poisson Model to Nineteenth-Century Europe. *American Political Science Review* 69:859-70.

Merritt, R. L., and Clark, C. M. 1977. An Example of Data Use: Mail Flows in the European Balance of Power, 1890-1920. In *Problems of World Modeling: Political and Social Implications,* K. W. Deutsch, B. Fritsch, H. Jaguaribe and A. S. Markovits (eds.), Cambridge, Mass.: Ballinger, pp. 169-205.

Midlarsky, M. I. 1981. Equilibria in the Nineteenth-Century Balance-of-Power System. *American Journal of Political Science,* 25:270-296.

_____. 1978. Analyzing Diffusion and Contagion Effects: The Urban Disorders of the 1960s. *American Political Science Review* 72: 996-1008.

_____. 1970. Mathematical Models of Instability and a Theory of Diffusion. *International Studies Quarterly* 14:60-84.

Midlarsky, M. I.; Crenshaw, M.; and Yoshida, F. 1980. Why Violence Spreads: The Contagion of International Terrorism. *International Studies Quarterly* 24:262-298.

Most, B. A. and Starr, H. 1980. Diffusion, Reinforcement, Geopolitics, and the Spread of War. *American Political Science Review* 74:932-946.

Penson, L. M. 1943. The New Course in English Foreign Policy, 1892-1902. *Transactions of the Royal Historical Society,* 4th ser. 25:121-38.

Pradt, D. 1800. *La Prusse et sa Neutralité.* London: G. Cowie.

Singer, J. D., and Small, M. 1966. Formal Alliances, 1815-1939: A Quantitative Description. *Journal of Peace Research* 3:1-32.

_____. 1968. Alliance Aggregation and the Onset of War. In *Quantitative International Politics: Insights and Evidence,* J. D. Singer (ed.), New York: The Free Press.

Siverson, R. M., and Duncan, G. T. 1976. Stochastic Models of International Alliance Initiation, 1885-1965. In *Mathematical Models in International Relations,* D. A. Zinnes and J. V. Gillespie, (eds.), New York: Praeger, pp. 110-31.

Small, M., and Singer, J. D. 1969. Formal Alliances, 1816-1965: An Extension of the Basic Data. *Journal of Peace Research* 6:257-82.

ter Haar, D. 1954. *Elements of Statistical Mechanics.* New York: Rinehart.

Tolman, R. C. 1962. *The Principles of Statistical Mechanics.* Oxford: Oxford Univ. Press.

Vattel, E. 1870. *The Law of Nations,* Vol. III. Philadelphia: T. and J. W. Johnson.

Zinnes, D. A. 1967. An Analytical Study of the Balance of Power Theories. *Journal of Peace Research* 4:270-88.

4

THE THEORY of PROTRACTED SOCIAL CONFLICT and the CHALLENGE of TRANSFORMING CONFLICT SITUATIONS

Edward E. Azar

INTRODUCTION

Over the past thirty years, empirically-oriented students of conflict, in their efforts to find a proper methodology, have tended to focus conflict theory on interaction without closely examining each actor's unique historical experiences—on the benefits and costs of conflict to the "topdogs" as opposed to the "underdogs" and other victims, and on "management" rather than on *transformation* of conflict situations.

It was natural for conflict researchers to focus on conflict between big powers during the "strategic balance of terror" era, but now that both the location and character of the bulk of international conflict has gravitated overwhelmingly toward the Third World, so too must the focus of conflict research shift. Perhaps a preoccupation with conflicts between major powers has caused researchers to shy away from a very common but extremely complex and all-absorbing type of conflict—protracted social conflict.

I would like to posit an alternative methodology, a richer paradigm of conflict that takes substantive realities into account. This chapter briefly describes my own view of protracted social conflict. The discussion covers the characteristics and properties that distinguish protracted social conflict from inter-state conflict, as well as the theoretical logic of conflict. My argument posits a structural relationship between conflict and the international system, specifically with international stratification. Thus conflict becomes linked to issues of inequitable distribution both between and within societies.

Finally, the implications of protracted social conflict for peace research will be examined. The complexities of these conflicts make it difficult for peace researchers and conflict managers to untangle the various interconnected factors. In fact, acceptance of protracted social conflict as a relevant paradigm in many Third World conflicts has grave implications for the utility of conflict management. Too often these strategies have dealt only with the *symptoms* of overt conflict without coming to grips with the far more difficult problems of structural ine-quity and violence. As such, conflict managers have focused on conflict containment, suppression, or abatement. Such short-sighted palliatives often result in system breakdown as we have seen in Iran, Lebanon, and Nicaragua. As Cioffi-Revilla's description of the international system demonstrates, protracted social conflict is very destabilizing, and con-flict management strategies are inadequate for dealing with it. But if we intend to intervene in and manage protracted social conflicts, then we need to describe and explain their nature and adopt more realistic assumptions about the roles and limits of power and intervention in in-ternational relations. The chapter concludes with suggestions regarding transformation of protracted social conflict situations, specifically with reference to the linkage between conflict theory and development theory.

EMPIRICAL CONFLICT THEORY

The Superpower Bias

Empirical conflict theory has made some significant contributions toward understanding inter-state behavior, but it has ignored systematic analysis of the structural sources of conflict and cooperation between and within states (Wallace, 1972). Western scholars have em-phasized escalation, strategic interactions, breakpoints, crises, and con-tainment of violent conflict—primarily from the viewpoint of the superpowers. The minimal attention paid to small actors in the literature has tended to focus only on how small states as targets affect superpowers rather than as actors in their own right. Consequently, there has been very little progress in our knowledge about demographic, ethnic, cultural, religious, and linguistic aspects which are endemic in nonwestern nation-states.

Contemporary conflict theory has generalized the historical ex-perience of European inter-state politics. This state system was characterized by specific historical features—well-defined geographical and cultural boundaries that were configured by endogenous forces, sizable populations with appropriate natural endowments, and a historical sense of national identity—conditions not at all universal in the developing world. Yet this Eurocentric world-view continues to hinder the realization that two-thirds of the world's states are small, destitute, poorly defined, and vulnerable to an international system over which they have practically no control. The attempt to apply a Eurocentric world-view to a radically different environment was bound to falter.

The most glaring error has been the failure to link *conflict* theory with *development* theory. Without such a link, it is impossible to understand these trends. The best either conflict or development theory can do is to describe trends in what are assumed to be independent social arenas. It is not possible, for example, to comprehend the grinding nature and psychological cost of perpetual conflict on the people of the Middle East if one focuses exclusively on the Arab-Israeli wars. Without exploring the relationship between conflict on the one hand— and development factors (structural inequality, population dynamics, resource maldistribution, poorly planned and executed development projects, ethnic struggle, and colonial experience) on the other—one cannot fully understand the dynamics of war or peace in the region.

The rationale behind the superpower bias is plausible: the role, power (actual and potential), responsibilities, and privileges of superpowers in the contemporary international state system far exceed those of smaller nations. Superpowers set the international agenda and determine, both directly and indirectly, the parameters, types, and intensity of interactions in the international system. According to some conflict theories, the rest of the world provides arenas for superpower competition and consists of states that are merely clients who benefit or suffer commensurately with their superpower sponsors.

If superpower politics are the only ones that count, then the empirical conflict researcher has been quite justified in assuming over the past three decades that in order to affect global change one should focus on the superpowers—their behavior, their alliances, and their ability to manage and contain conflict situations. This assumption, however, poses serious problems. Some conflicts are not easily muted by the availability of resources, instruments of violence, projection of power, and the like. Some conflicts are so deep and intransigent in the "short run" that containment or "management" is of little value. Furthermore, the assumption that the superpowers can achieve containment is in itself misguided. They can contain the *scope* or *intensity* of conflicts to a limited degree, but they are not always capable of *transforming* a conflict situation, even when they wish to. This is not to say that the superpowers have lost their ability to contain, manipulate, mute, amplify, or dominate the various regional political and economic conflicts. I am only suggesting that the complexity of protracted social conflict has reduced the effectiveness of superpower intervention.

Research

There is another problem with contemporary conflict research. In the most general terms, empirical conflict theory has focused on overt conflict behavior rather than on its structural roots. As a strategy for understanding this behavior, researchers have broken up the conflict process, hoping to derive a more profound understanding through fragmentation and division of labor. This strategy has had two unfortunate effects on the study of conflict:

> *a.* attention has focused on describing and predicting increasingly limited aspects of the conflict process; and
> *b.* primary communication is between people engaged in the same type of research, each having its own professional jargon and community of understanding; thus scholars in different research branches communicate little, if at all.

As a result, empirical findings have tended to be trivial, especially from the viewpoint of the American foreign policy establishment. The depth of knowledge that might have been generated by pooling diverse research findings has so far not been produced. As a first step in this direction, I will attempt to define a new model of conflict, one which I feel integrates various foci of the different research communities.

PROTRACTED SOCIAL CONFLICT

Several writers have demonstrated that the incidence of conflict in the international system has risen since 1945, with the greatest increase occurring between 1956 and 1965. (See Azar, 1973; Eckhardt and Azar, 1978; Kende, 1971; Bouthoul and Carrere, 1976; Butterworth and Scranton, 1976.) COPDAB data indicate that since World War II domestic civil strife, regional crises, and overall international outbreaks of violence have averaged about thirty per annum. Over 90 percent of these conflicts have taken place in the Third World, and most have been protracted and social-ethnic, rather than strategic conflicts.

Using the conflict-years as a measure of a conflict's saliency, we have found that *overt* conflicts increased substantially in the early sixties and then tapered off after 1970. The increase between 1945 and 1972 appears to have been very sharp indeed, with the period 1945-1960 accounting for about 40 percent of the total global conflict in the post-World War II period, and 50 percent of all took place between 1961 and 1970. The data demonstrate that western and communist interventions in the Third World increased between 1945 and 1970 to such an extent that the United States and the USSR had become parties to most Third World disputes; however, overt (primarily military) conflicts and interventions have decreased significantly in the 1970s. This new development was also associated with an increased level of conflict in the Middle East and a decreased level in Asia, fewer international civil conflicts, and an overall reduction in western military intervention in conflict worldwide.

While these statistics refer to instances of overt violence, many of the conditions which precipitated these severe hostilities are ethnic/cultural/linguistic/economic exploitation or structural disequilibrium. Yet the linkages between these internal or international configurations and overt eruptions of violence have not been adequately examined by empirically-oriented students of conflict.

In several recent papers (Azar, 1979; Azar and Cohen, 1979; Azar et al., 1978) some colleagues and I have employed the term "protracted social conflict" to characterize those conflicts in which structural behavior (ethnic, religious, linguistic, economic) has affected overt hostile behavior (interaction), creating a complicated causal network that makes these conflicts difficult to "solve."

It should be emphasized that internal domestic power struggles between military factions or violent inter-state clashes over border issues do *not* constitute protracted social conflicts. These conflicts are not "purely" domestic or international. It does not require much thought to unearth a myriad of examples: Iran, Lebanon, Cyprus, Ethiopia, Nicaragua, etc. Nor are they restricted solely to the Third World as the strife in Ireland illustrates. Also note that descriptive terms used to characterize protracted social conflict such as "civil strife," "low intensity conflict," and "continuing revolution" are no longer useful because quantitative social science has progressed in different directions over the past few decades. For example, "low intensity conflict" emphasizes the vertical intensity of a dispute rather than its longitudinal protractedness.

In instances where structural behavior affects overt hostile behavior, tension reduction seems to resist even the most persistent efforts of well-intentioned mediators. When tension reduction is achieved on one level of the dispute, another will flare up, almost as if by hydraulic action. This characteristic creates disputes that extend over long periods

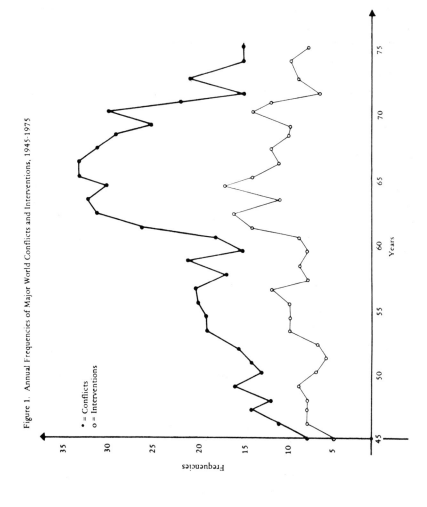

Figure 1. Annual Frequencies of Major World Conflicts and Interventions, 1945-1975

• = Conflicts
o = Interventions

86

Table 1

SELECTED PROTRACTED CONFLICTS

Conflict Actors	Years	External Parties
Kashmir (India, Pakistan) and India-Pakistan	1947-49 and many years of tension since 1947	China
Arab-Israeli	1948-78	UK, USA, USSR and many others
China-Taiwan	1949-78	USA and others
North Korea-South Korea	1950-78	USA, NATO, USSR, China and others
Cyprus (Turkish-Greek)	Pre - and post - 1962	NATO and others
Trieste (Italy-Yugoslavia)	1947-52 and after	
Cambodia-South Vietnam	Since 1949	USA, China and others
North Vietnam-Laos	1953-57 and after	
Somalia-Ethiopia	1961 to present	Arab states, Western and Eastern bloc states
Lebanon (internal and inter-Arab)	1945 to present	Arab, USA, USSR, France and others
Northern Ireland	Especially since 1970	UK
Sino-Soviet	Since the 1950's but especially since 1963	
Berlin (West Germany, East Germany and NATO-Warsaw Pact)	1948 to present	

Notes:

South Africa, Rhodesia and many such ethnic conflicts fall within this category of protracted social conflicts. We give the above examples in order to illustrate the point established earlier in the paper.

FIGURE 2

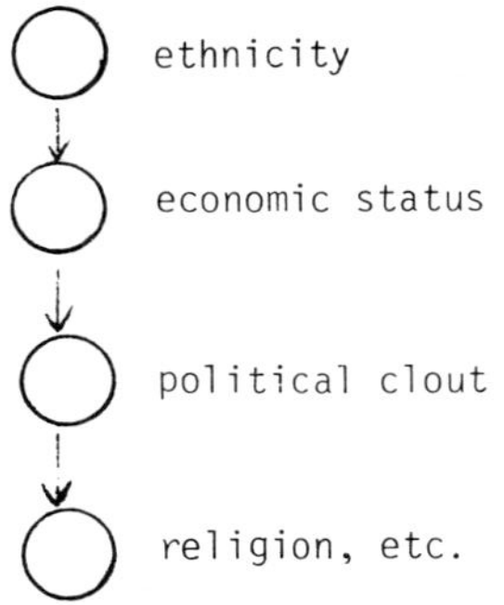

SINGLE DIRECTION IMPACT

ethnicity

economic status

political clout

religion, etc.

Instead, it looks like this:

DUAL DIRECTION IMPACT;
Multidimensional linkage

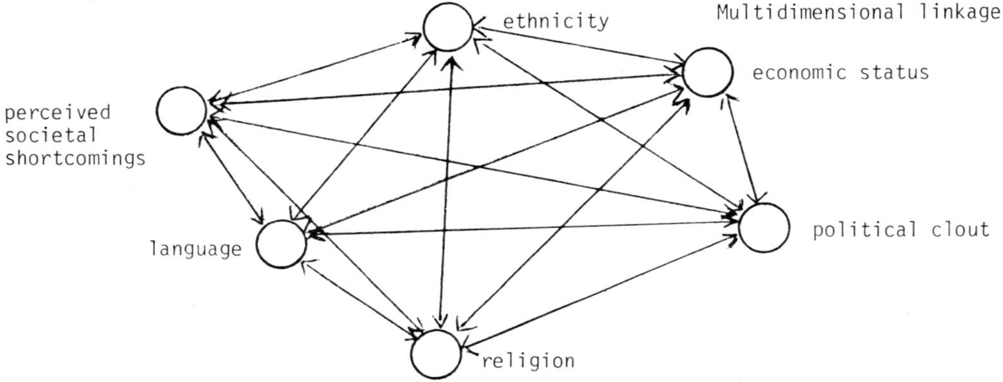

economic status

political clout

ethnicity

religion

perceived
societal
shortcomings

language

of time and become all-consuming for the populations in question. Protracted social conflicts exhibit inertia produced by structural deformity. The frequency and intensity of their periodic eruptions fluctuates. Characterized by hostile interactions with sporadic outbreaks of war, protracted social conflicts lack distinct termination points and spill over into all aspects of societal life. Because these conflicts involve whole societies, their stakes are very high and the issues become the determining criteria in the definition of national identity and social solidarity. These conflicts are not terminated by explicit decisions, although cessation of overt violence may defuse tensions somewhat. They tend to linger on in time and gradually cool down, become transformed, or wither away. Hence management becomes complicated precisely because protracted social conflicts are not specific events at distinct points in time; they are processes.

Protracted social conflicts do not permit change in the fundamental grievances and continually reduce the chances for dealing with settlement issues. They tend to generate, reinforce, and intensify mutual images of deception. They tend to increase the likelihood of confusion in the direct and indirect communications between the parties and their allies. They increase the anxieties of the parties to the conflict, and foster tension and conflict-maintenance strategies. In a protracted conflict situation, the conflict becomes an arena for redefining issues rather than a means for adjudicating them; it is therefore futile to look for any ultimate resolution because the conflict process itself becomes the *source* rather than the *outcome* of policy.

Structural Victimization, Protracted Conflict, and the Role of Ethnicity
The next stage in defining protracted social conflict is the search for structural determinants of hostile behavior. In order to pinpoint these determinants, I divide social structure into three distinct components: economic structure, political structure, and ideology. The *economic structure* of a society is determined by the stage of development of its productive forces and its position within the international division of labor. *Political structure* is built on the relative access to power of contending social forces. *Ideology* is the conduit through which economic and political interactions shape images and perceptions of social forces; ideology organizes society in the economic and political arenas.

It seems that the peripheral integration of developing countries into the international economic system has produced conditions which facilitate the rise and perpetuation of protracted social conflicts. These conditions include a growing structure of economic inequality, the inefficacy of contemporary models of economic development, and a bureaucratic authoritarianism enabling the state apparatus to cope with the economic crises resulting from that integration into the global economy. Restoration of equality of economic opportunity is essential for resolving protracted social conflicts.

Inequality in the *social* structure is largely responsible for overt hostile behavior, especially in protracted social conflicts. It is the product of political and economic inequality and ideological domination of one social group over another. Political inequality is the asymmetrical distribution of political power among social forces and the domination of the state apparatus by one class or social group. Ideology legitimizes this differential access to power, and attempts to stabilize this social structure through rationalization. The sum of these three inequalities is a situation of structural victimization that is directly responsible for the emergence and endurance of protracted social conflicts.

Such inequality usually takes the form of ethnic discrimination. Sectoral, factional, and regional imbalances coincide with the existence of multi-ethnic countries. Ethnicity becomes a mode of political organization and a source of ideological expression. Structural victimization is perceived to affect some groups disproportionately or to benefit other groups. It is at this juncture of actual physical and psychological deprivation that structural victimization bursts into hostile and violent actions and interactions.

Group identity formation and protracted social conflicts are inextricably linked. Ethnicity is an acute awareness that there is a bond between people of similar culture, language, religion, beliefs, customs, habits, and—most important—life perspectives. The shared perceptions encompass all of life's core values and issues. This bond transcends class differences because it embodies central immutable characteristics which cannot be discarded like class status can. It leaves an indelible mark of identity on each of its heirs. By universalizing a set of distinct social interactions for its members, ethnicity becomes an expression of uniqueness vis-a-vis others.

Ethnic groups are a natural outcome of an individual's need to structure reality and to belong to those who see reality similarly; an individual is likely to join a group because it fulfills a desire to achieve oneness with cultural peers. Security from the vagaries of the outside is a commonality shared by all members regardless of the group. Within the context of protracted social conflict the victimization which affects each individual is buttressed by the fact that the external reality is perceived as being set against the group collectively, not against the individual directly affected. Thus security even in the midst of calamity is assured by the maintenance of group ties. (As a digression, it is not assumed that all members of a group use exactly the same formula in coming up with an assessment of their environment. What is being assumed is that the ingredients used—beliefs, values, images—are markedly similar. So there is diversity in both the means and ends of the group's membership but *not in their assessment of their victimization.)* The linkage between their primary socialization and their appreciation of external reality assumes paramount importance.

Ethnicity, then, is a crucial ingredient of the tragedy of protracted social conflict. It colors the significance of all social interactions and imputes suspicious behavior to all outsiders. When both parties to a conflict attribute malevolent motivations to each other, it breeds a vicious circle of self-fulfilling prophecies. Intercommunal hatred is passed from generation to generation through primary socialization. When group identity is assumed at birth, one of its integral components—mutual hatred—is also inherited.

Under conditions not marked by protracted social conflict, intergenerational assimilation might proceed without backlash. But the structural victimization that plagues every ethnic/cultural group is brought to the fore by social conflict. Group identity, a cluster of most deeply-held values, is impervious to rational change. Eruptions of violence appear disjointed and discrete because they are sparked by the continuing presence of cultural identification and intercommunal antagonism. Thus ethnicity filters reality and further restricts the ability of the state or outside parties to control, subjugate, or sublimate the conflict, and thwarts the capability of the state to ameliorate these eruptions.

Such a configuration renders the standard analytic tools of social scientists inadequate. Their analyses treat each violent eruption discretely and, as a result, they force analysts to seek extraordinary explanations. But the pervasiveness of the imagery held by each ethnic group defines for the membership when it is most likely to be threatened. Although the eruptions of violence appear to be disjointed and discrete, underlying them is the continuing presence of cultural identification. Violence might manifest itself over an intercommunal argument regarding the exact representation in government as it did in Cyprus during the early sixties, or it might manifest itself in the distribution of services, of land, of employment opportunities, of leisure opportunities, of artistic or cultural expression. In short, conflict might erupt over a whole range of interactions that constitute daily life. Conflict might be controlled, subjugated, or sublimated and expressed in turn as upward mobility or in "slippage," but it nonetheless reappears under different guises.

Since interactions between communes establish the fuel for identity formations, a protracted social conflict remains in a state of flux, forever changing in its manifestations. The implications for conflict theory, research, and resolution are explored in the final section.

Implications for Theory

The inherent inertia of protracted social conflict can be specified within fairly accurate and useful limits. The interconnected nature of the various structural factors (political, economic, ethnic, religious, linguistic) is what makes protracted social conflicts so devastatingly unresolvable. It is impossible to isolate each issue and resolve it separately, because each issue/sector of the conflict is linked to the others at a number of different levels. This means that each new factor compounds the complexity of the conflict in an unexpected manner because it tends to become linked with *every* other factor. If the conflict were comprised of issues with only one dimensional link, it would look like figure 2.

Furthermore, the final aggregate of the conflict's various factors is not necessarily equivalent to the sum of each one measured individually, because of the multidimensional nature of factor linkages. Two factors, one hostile and one peaceful, may neutralize each other. By the same token two seemingly harmless and neutral elements may create an unanticipated combustion of hostility. The multidimensionality of structural links and conflict augmentation results in inertia: the resiliency of protracted social conflict stems in part from the interconnectedness of these structural factors. The resolution of any given issue/sector of dispute is not necessarily absolute and final. It can flare up again precisely because it is inseparable from the other conflict sectors, each of which has its own repercussions on the "resolved" sector.

Systems with high inertia levels such as protracted social conflicts are much less affected by environmental interventions than those with low inertia levels. These high inertia systems are ultra-stable; that is, they resist change, even when the deviations from equilibrium are fairly strong and frequent.

If protracted social conflicts are viewed as inertial systems, we can make a connection between protracted social conflict and the "normal

Table 2

CONFLICT OCCURRENCES BY REGIONS/TYPE
BASED ON AZAR'S DATA

(A list of 641 major conflict events was used to generate 265 major conflicts
in the world between 1945/6 and 1975. When 94 coups and 8 large-scale riots
were subtracted from this list, 163 major conflicts (primarily protracted)
remained. The conflicts below are grouped by region and type).

Region	Conflict-Years	Intervention-Years
Europe (N=31)	5%	6%
Latin America (N=25)	10%	4%
Middle East (N=14)	16%	24%
North America (N=5)	5%	3%
Black Africa (N=36)	21%	20%
Asia (N=13)	16%	17%
Southeast Asia (N=12)	27%	26%
	100%	100%

Type		
Civil	44%	20%
International	29%	26%
Civil-International	27%	54%
	100%	100%

Notes:

N=...after the region names indicate the number of nations in each region.

Conflict-Year is the number of years during which the conflict has taken place.
It is the life-span of the conflict. Some conflicts last 30 years and some last
a few months.

Intervention-Year is the number of years in which non-primary parties to the
conflict were part of the conflict, incited it or kept fuelling it.

relations range" concept (Azar, 1972). In other words, the inertia of these conflicts is what allows a familiar routine and "normal" inter-nation interaction to materialize. If it were not for this property, normal international relations ranges would not be distinguishable. The higher the inertia of a conflict, the lower the entropy of the normal relations range and the sharper it will look. Obviously, these properties improve our explanatory and forecasting skills. If a protracted social conflict has higher inertia, it can be predicted to follow Markov's model.[1]

Intervention and Management Implications

There are basically two relevant orientations toward conflict and change—the activist peace researcher approach and the bureaucratic "manager" approach. Both look for points at which the conflict system can be intercepted. Both attempt to identify—through careful, precise, and "objective" empirical study—all the relevant intervention points in a conflict process. But, generally speaking, they differ in goals. The peace researcher intervenes in order to reduce both behavioral and structural violence properties of the system. The peace researcher wants a transformation of the conflict situation; the bureaucratic manager's first priority is to control the immediate situation. The "manager" wants to discover how violence can be contained and conflict spillover arrested. In the long run, such control may well enhance the conflict's perpetuation rather than alleviate it. Stated in more extreme terms, governmental managers are "topdog" oriented. They rarely exhibit concern for the "underdogs" or victims of conflict.

Interventionists as a whole have shown interest in crisis or semi-crisis situations whenever tension and violence escalate beyond normal levels. Both peace researchers and managers over the past three decades have tended to generate careful and precise findings about inter-nation crisis behavior in order to show how crisis dynamics might be frustrated, if necessary or useful to the powerful (cf. Young, 1977). For students of protracted social conflicts, the exclusive focus on crises is a poor normative and scientific strategy. It has some drawbacks even for topdogs. While the preoccupation with crises is laudable, it is also unfortunate. The effects are felt not only when violence erupts—individual and societal conditions are aggravated daily by continual victimization and resource waste. Furthermore, because new hostile goals are generated on a regular basis, attempts at settlement and change are undermined. Hence the cumulative effects of protracted social conflicts are probably even more detrimental to their victims than those of short-term, one-shot crises (as defined by the superpowers). While useful for certain

94

conflict situations, the traditional crisis focus (as designed and implemented from a superpower perspective) is not necessarily applicable to protracted social conflicts, since protracted social conflict is in itself a perpetual crisis and requires continuous action if correction or transformation is to be achieved.

The two schools of thought have overemphasized the concept of "manageability" which led them to investigate those limited aspects of conflict that interested the superpowers or suited their needs. Although some conflicts are in fact "manageable," these limited cases involve symmetrically-balanced states, resolution of isolated grievances, and short-term flare-ups without associated long-term memories.

Protracted social conflicts are different, but transformation is possible if it is based on a broader orientation: (a) protracted social conflict is a *societal* problem for all those parties involved in it; (b) crisis-mentality intervention is not sufficient for transformation of these conflicts; and (c) structural development is the most powerful remedy for protracted social conflict worldwide.

Protracted Social Conflict: Links between Conflict and Development Theories

Both dimensions of protracted social conflicts (inter-state strategic and social/structural) cannot be fully understood or dealt with without linking them to national, regional, and international development and to world structure. In order to make such a linkage successfully, development must be defined as community organization in response to change in the social and physical environments. Organization here refers to the structure of interdependencies between the economic, political, technological, and ideational/valuative systems which, in a broad sense, constitutes the community. The purpose of a development plan, therefore, must be the reorganization of this structure so that the community's capacity as the mediator between a human population and its environment is improved. Contemporary developmental thought is unable to meet this requirement because, in its desire to discover a simpler or more "elegant" solution, it tends to ignore these complex interdependencies and to produce instead policy recommendations that are theoretically appropriate but pragmatically inapplicable.

With few exceptions (e.g., Goulet, 1981), development analysis of all ideological colors tends to consider development isomorphic to growth in the economic sector. Growth models are comforting to political elites because they hold the hope of general improvement without necessarily involving large-scale reorganization. Of course, growth in the productive sector, especially in nations with rapidly expanding populations, is crucial for maintaining the physical quality of life. However, the assumption that such growth will uniformly eliminate social conflict is clearly inaccurate. A careful analysis of societal structure and community-specific social relations is essential if linkages between economic growth, social peace, and protracted social conflict are to be understood.

Societies experiencing protracted social conflicts are usually characterized by poverty, inequality, police state regimes, acute problems of population growth and overt violence—all interacting in a vicious circle. Careful extrapolations into the future reveal that the condition of these victimized societies could worsen even further. One solution to this historical dilemma is to coordinate global, regional, and national development to address the roots of social conflict. If development plans and development theory are at a crossroads, the linkage between conflict theory and development theory could be the most important intellectual challenge for students of protracted social conflict.

At the expense of precision, I will venture to suggest a way to meet this challenge. (A detailed discussion can be found in Azar, *Peace Amidst Development,* 1979.)

I would suggest that the core goal of any meaningful development plan must be the reduction of inequality. Growth in the economic sector without a corresponding reduction of inequality seems somewhat lacking in moral justification. Furthermore, I would argue that it is doomed to fail as hyper-development of the economic system increasingly isolates it from social organization. These conditions will precipitate social breakdown.

It is useful to conceive of this process in terms of the level of "structural victimization" produced by the social system.[2] Structural victimization is the condition of rank inequality and disequilibrium in the system which has emerged as a by-product of the historical development of a specific social system. It is a reality that permeates every level of social existence. An individual is victimized whenever a beneficial action or choice is structurally denied him. Significantly, the victim need not be consciously aware of the source or the occurrence of his victimization in order for it to take place (Fanon, 1963; Sennett and Cobb, 1972). An example from American history is the de facto denial of civil and human rights to black Americans as a consequence of the institution which originally imported them to America—slavery.

The concept of structural victimization will be useful to link development and social conflict in general, specifically in societies currently undergoing protracted conflicts. If inequality persists and increases to intolerable levels, behavioral manifestations of conflict will be induced. Only the elimination of the roots of victimization will ultimately reduce outbreaks of violence and create conditions for stable and long-term peace.

NOTES

1. This point was suggested to me by my colleague, Claudio Cioffi-Revilla, University of Illinois.

2. Marx's work on alienation under the capitalist mode of production (Ollman, 1971) is an early example of this kind of analysis from which we can learn much about what to do and what not to do. Hirsch's (1976) work is an outstanding example.

REFERENCES

Amin, S. 1974. *Accumulation on a World Scale.* New York: Monthly Review Press.

Azar, E. E. 1979. Peace Amidst Development: A Conceptual Agenda for Conflict and Peace Research. *International Interactions* 6:2.

_____. 1972. Conflict Escalation and Conflict Reduction in an International Crisis: Suez, 1956. *J of Conflict Resolution* 16:2.

Azar, E. E., and Cohen, S. 1979. Peace as Crisis and War as Status-Quo: The Arab-Israeli Conflict Environment. *International Interactions* 6:2.

Azar, E. E., and Eckhardt, W. 1979. Major Military Conflicts and Interventions, 1965-1979. *Peace Research* 11:4.

Azar, E. E.; Jureidini, P.; and McLaurin, R. 1978. Protracted Social Conflict. *J of Palestine Studies* 8:1 (Autumn).

Barth, R. 1969. *Ethnic Groups and Boundaries.* Oslo: Bergen.

Bendix, R. 1964. *Nation Building.* Berkeley: Univ. of California Press.

Choucri, N., and North, R. 1975. *Nations in Conflict.* San Francisco: W. H. Freeman.

Coser, L. 1957. *Functions of Social Conflict.* Glencoe IL: Free Press.

Dalaader, H. 1973. Building Consociational Nations. In *Building States and Nations,* Eisenstadt and Rokkan, (eds.). Beverly Hills, CA: Sage.

Davies, J. C. 1962. Towards a Theory of Revolution. *American Sociological Review* 27.

Deutsch, K. 1953. *Nationalism and Social Communications.* Cambridge, Mass: MIT Press.

Easterlin, R.; Ranis, G.; Morishima, M.; and Hoselitz, B. 1968. Economic Growth. *International Encyclopedia of the Social Sciences* 4:395-429.

Eisenstadt, S., and Rokkan, R. 1973. *Building States and Nations,* Vol I & II. Beverly Hills, CA: Sage.

Emmanuel, A. 1972. *Unequal Exchange.* New York: Monthly Review Press.

Enloe, C. 1980. *Ethnic Soldiers: Security in Divided Societies.* Athens, GA: Univ. of Georgia Press.

Fanon, F. 1963. *The Wretched of the Earth.* New York: Grove Press.

Farah, N., and Eid, S. H. 1979. Interaction Between Variations in Socio-Economic Indicators of Development and Some Population Growth Measures. *Planning Techniques Unit Research Papers.* Cairo: Population and Family Planning Board.

Frank, A. G. 1972. The Development of Underdevelopment. In *Dependence and Underdevelopment.* New York: Doubleday.

Galtung, J. 1971. Structural Theory of Imperialism. *J of Peace Research*:5.

_____. 1969. Violence, Peace and Peace Research. *J of Peace Research*:3.

_____. 1969. A Structural Theory of Aggression. *J of Peace Research*:2.

Goulet, D. 1971. *The Cruel Choice.* New York: Atheneum.

Gurr, T. 1969. A Comparative Study of Civil Strife. In *Violence in America,* H. D. Graham and T. Gurr (eds.). Washington, D.C.: National Commission on the Causes and Prevention of Violence.

Hammond, P. 1975. *Cold War and Detente.* New York: Harcourt, Brace, Jovanovich.

Himes, D. 1980. *Conflict and Conflict Management.* Athens, GA: Univ. of Georgia Press.

Hoetnik, H. 1974. National Identity and Somatic Norm Image. In *Ethnicity and Nation-Building,* W. Bell and W. Freeman (eds.). Beverly Hills, CA: Sage.

Huntington, S. 1968. *Political Order in Changing Societies.* New Haven: Yale Univ. Press.

Kelman, Herbert, 1978. Israel and Palestinians: Psychological Prerequisites for Mutual Recognition. *AFSC Report.*

Kende, I. 1978. Wars of Ten Years: 1967-1976. *J of Peace Research* 15:3.

Kriesberg, L. 1973. *The Sociology of Social Conflict.* New Jersey: Prentice Hall.

Lenski, G. 1966. *Power and Privilege.* New York: McGraw-Hill.

Mack, R., and Snyder, R. C. 1957. The Analysis of Social Conflict: Towards an Overview and Synthesis. *J of Conflict Resolution* 1:1.

Mead, M. 1958. *Israel and Problem of Identity.* New York: Theodore Herzl Foundation.

Ollman, B. 1971. *Marx's Conception of Man in Capitalist Society.* Cambridge:Cambridge Univ. Press.

Palmer, R., and Parson, N. 1977. *The Roots of Rural Poverty in Central and Southern Africa.* Berkeley: Univ. of California Press.

Said, M. 1981. Integration as a Mode of Ethnic Conflict Resolution in Africa. *International Interactions* 8:4, pp 349-72.

Sennett, R., and Cobb, J. 1972. *The Hidden Injuries of Class.* New York: Knopf.

Sewell, J. 1977. *Agenda for Action: 1977.* New York: Overseas Development Corp.

Tinbergen, J. 1976 *RIO: Reshaping the International Order.* New York: Dutton.

Wallace, M. 1972. Radical Critiques of Peace Research: An Exposition and Interpretation. *Peace Research Review* 4:4.

Wallerstein, I. 1974. *The Modern World-System: Capitalist Agriculture and the Origins of the European World Economy in the 16th Century.* New York:New York Academic Press.

_____. 1960. Ethnicity and National Integration in West Africa. *Cahiers d'Etudes Africaines* 1:3.

Wirth, L. 1945. The Problem of Minority Groups. In *The Science of Man in the World Crisis,* R. Lonton, (ed.). New York: Columbia Univ. Press.

Young, Robert A., Ed. 1977. International Crisis: Progress and Prospects for Applied Forecasting and Management. *International Studies Quarterly* 21:1.

5

A MODEL OF SPORADIC CONFLICT

Philip A. Schrodt

INTRODUCTION

The concept of protracted conflict (Azar et al., 1978, 1979) is useful in International Relations and Comparative Politics, since increasingly violent conflict is occurring in areas characterized by long-standing disputes that defy resolution. Among nations, the hostilities between Arabs and Israelis, Iran and Iraq, India and Pakistan, the Koreas, and USSR and China are current examples of this; the Franco-German border disputes which led to wars in 1870, 1914 and 1939 are others. Within nations, long-standing ethnic disputes have produced protracted conflict in Lebanon, Kurdistan, Sri Lanka, the Philippines, Malaysia, Central America, Belgium, and Canada.

Protracted conflict challenges international relations theory in at least two ways. First, most international relations theory assumes that the international system and the nations within it are characterized by peace, with violent conflict an unusual situation. In protracted conflict situations, conflict becomes the norm, with peace the exception. Second, the fact that protracted conflict continues over a long period of time would imply that some mechanism is maintaining it. The understandable emphasis in most international relations theory has been on maintaining peace (e.g., through deterrence or conflict resolution), but nonetheless there appear to exist stable mechanisms which maintain *conflict*. Conflict mechanisms are distinct from crisis mechanisms since conflicts persist over periods of decades while crises end after a period of weeks or months.

Support for this research was granted by National Science Foundation Grant SES-8025053. I would like to thank Bruce Moon, Dina Zinnes and an anonymous referee for helpful comments on the model.

Another characteristic of protracted conflict is the occurrence of short-term "spikes" of high levels of conflict. These spikes are characterized by abnormally high amounts of violence; they are referred to as wars when international and as riots, revolts, revolutions, civil wars, or disturbances when domestic. Two characteristic spike patterns are illustrated in figures 1 and 2—international conflict in the European system and peasant revolts in Japan, respectively. The outbreak of wars in the Middle East in 1956, 1967, 1973 and 1982 are spikes of conflict, as are outbreaks of racial violence in the United States or Sri Lanka. Conflict spikes are found in most conflict data sets and are usually identified as a specific historical event (e.g., World War I, Detroit riots, Lebanese civil war).

A conflict spike is a specific form of system breakdown. The question pursued here is whether the system is breaking down, or if we are looking at a different mode of behavior in the same system. Ideally, spikes of conflict should be part of a continuous dynamic process, since the actors in the system usually do not change dramatically during the transition from low to high conflict. France and Germany in September, 1914, were the same nations—in terms of institutions, population, history and culture—as the France and Germany of June, 1914; yet they were behaving very differently.

The model presented in this chapter describes a mechanism by which the apparent "breakdown" in a system evidenced by the sudden increase in the level of conflict may in fact be the result of a specific type of protracted conflict situation. This model differs from earlier work on protracted conflict in that the dynamic mechanism controlling the conflict causes the system to appear peaceful; in most previous work, protracted conflict situations are assumed to result in low-level but visible amounts of conflict. I would argue that the same conflict mechanism continues to operate over long periods of time without the conflict being resolved, even if that conflict is not always measurable.

The model also differs from previous work on the peace-war transition, which usually assumes that some explicit "breakdown" in the peacekeeping mechanisms of the system must occur in order for war (or high levels of conflict) to occur. For example, most simulations deal with "peace" and "war" using separate mechanisms, and contain some type of stochastic element or decision rule to transfer between those mechanisms. In contrast, the model proposed here utilizes the same mechanism to generate low levels of conflict and sporadic occurrences of high levels of conflict. In short, a system which appears to be essentially peaceful with occasional breakdowns resulting in high levels

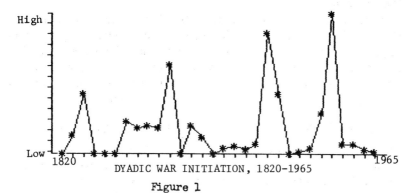

DYADIC WAR INITIATION, 1820-1965

Figure 1

Source: Davis, Duncan and Siverson, 1978

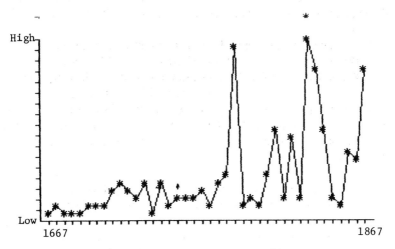

PEASANT UPRISINGS JAPAN, 1667-1867

Figure 2

Source and Data: Borton, 1968

103

of conflict may in fact be governed by a specific type of protracted conflict mechanism.

In an earlier paper (Schrodt, 1981), I suggested that a logistic (Verhulst-Pearl-Reed) model for conflict containing a lagged term might account for this type of behavior. This chapter extends that analysis to take into account the behavior of the equation when a random perturbation is also present, and discusses the problems of empirically estimating the parameters of such an equation.

A DYNAMIC MECHANISM FOR SPIKED CONFLICT

The conflict model presented in Schrodt (1981) was originally intended to model situations of persistent conflict, such as those observed in Middle East events data by Azar and others (Azar and Cohen, 1979; Azar, Jureidini and McLaurin, 1978). The model hypothesized that there are two groups which affect the level of international conflict—nationalists and internationalists. Nationalists are individuals who benefit by *increased* conflict. They might benefit financially (e.g., trade barriers, military expenditures), or simply be xenophobic and support increased conflict because of perceived theats to their security. Internationalists, in contrast, are individuals who benefit from *reduced* levels of conflict (for example, increased international trade or decreases in military expenditures), or oppose conflict for philosophical reasons.

The dynamic model is based on the assumption that each group has a preferred level of conflict. This preferred level will be designated N for the nationalists and I for the internationalists. When the actual level of conflict, c(t), is different from the desired level of one of the groups, that group will exert political pressure to raise or lower the level until it returns to their desired state. The amount of pressure exerted is assumed to be proportional to the distance between the actual level and the desired level, i.e.,

Nationalist pressure to increase conflict = g*[N-c(t)]
Internationalist pressure to decrease conflict = h*[c(t)-I],

where g and h are constants which give the relative power of each group. The aggregate change in the level of conflict is assumed to be proportional to the sum of the pressures for change, and hence c(t) is governed by the differential equation:

$$dc/dt = c(t)*\{g*[N-c(t)]-h*[c(t)-I]\}. \tag{1.1}$$

It can be shown without difficulty that when $I < N$ the model will produce an equilibrium level of conflict at the level

$$N \quad \frac{(gN + hI)}{(g + h)} \quad I.$$

This equilibrium is stable for all levels of conflict, $c(t) > 0$, so if a random disturbance causes the level of conflict to go above or below the equilibrium, it will return there through the dynamics of the model. This model therefore demonstrates at least the basic characteristics of the protracted conflict situation.

In the process of exploring the behavior of the model, I experimentally introduced a lag into the response of the two groups, i.e., producing the difference-differential model

$$dc/dt = c(t)*\{g*[N-c(t-n)]-h*[e(t-i)-I]\}, \qquad (1.2)$$

where i and n give the time lag for the response of the two groups.

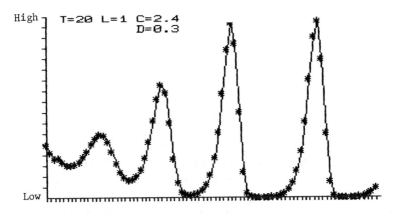

Spiked behavior pattern

Figure 3

105

These lags seem plausible since it is very unlikely that a political group reacts instantaneously to the conflict level; instead some delay is involved. As expected, for small values of g and h, the effect of this change was to cause the model to oscillate back to the equilibrium rather than returning monotonically.

For larger values of g and h, however, an unexpected behavior occurred. The simple oscillations gave way to a more complex "spiked" behavior, consisting of relatively long periods of almost no conflict separated by short periods of high levels of conflict. Figure 3 illustrates a typical pattern of spiked behavior. This type of conflict behavior is, if anything, more common in observed behavior than in the protracted conflict, and would be characteristic of any area where there are periodic "flare-ups" of conflict over time. Figures 1 and 2 give two examples of spiked behavior; several others will be suggested. Because of the importance of this type of behavior, the lagged model appeared to justify further investigation on its own merits.

DETERMINISTIC BEHAVIOR OF THE MODEL

In order to analyze the model more thoroughly, it is first convenient to reduce it to a simpler form. If we assume that the lag times are equal $(i = n)$, then the model reduces to an equation of the form

$$dx/dt = Cx(t) [1 - Dx(t-L)] \tag{2.1}$$

where

$$C = gN + hI$$

$$D = g + h.$$

Since this equation gives the basic form of the model, I will deal with it rather than the more complex form given above. The model is related to the finite-difference logistic model which has been extensively discussed by May (1976) and in all likelihood shares some of the "chaotic" features of that model under some choices of parameters. Unfortunately for empirical work, the model is underidentified in the sense that for any given pair of values for C and D, an infinite number of combinations of g, h, I, and N can be found which will produce the same C and D values.

There is no simple way to obtain a closed-form solution to (2.1). Hale (1971:156) provides an existence proof for a periodic solution to an equation similar to (2.1) but this is only an existence proof. Consequently, the analysis of the behavior of the equation will be done using numerical approximations.[1]

The first question is whether the spiked behavior is found for a broad or a limited set of parameter values. A set of empirical experiments was undertaken to map the behavior of the equation as a function of C and D at the unit lag, $L = 1$. The model was approximated using Euler's method with a differencing interval of $h = 0.01^2$ (see Ross, 1964:278). The initial value of x(t) was set at $x(t) = 10.0$ for $-L < t < 0$.

On the basis of the experiments, the value of D appears to make very little difference in the behavior of the solution. It has some effect on the magnitude of the oscillations and a small effect on their frequency, but does not affect whether or not they occur. That behavior is determined primarily by C in the range $0.1 < D < 5.0$. Table 1 summarizes the behavior of the solution as a function of C.

TABLE 1

Solution Form as a Function of C when L=1

C	Solution form
0.5	Stable, slight oscillation to equil.
1.0	Stable, oscillations to equilibrium
2.0	Spikey oscillations
3.0	Initial small oscillations, then spikes
4.0	Sharp spikes
5.0	Program crashes

---

* Parameters: x(0)=10.0; L=1; D=0.5

In general, the spiked behavior intensifies as C increases, with 2.0 being a rough breaking point at which conspicuously spiked behavior occurs. In this and later examples, high values of C were impossible to compute, due to round-off errors in the program; these occurred as the values of C went below $10 \frown -35$.[3]

In addition to inducing the formation of spiked behavior, the intensity of the maximum behavior increases as the value of C increases. In the higher values of C, the magnitude of the spikes is on the order of $10 \frown 2$. In the stable cases, x(t) settles down to its equilibrium value of 1/D. Changes in the initial value have little long-range impact in the equations tested.

The other parameter of interest is the lag time L. In general, increasing L seems to have two effects:

    a. The value of C sufficient to induce spikes decreases as L increases; and
    b. The frequency of spikes decreases dramatically as L increases.

Table 2 summarizes these results and gives the approximate values of C needed to induce the spiked behavior. Models with values of C below these critical points oscillate into the equilibrium without spiked behavior.

TABLE 2

Approximate Value of C needed to induce spikes and spike frequency as a function of L

L	Value of C needed to induce spikes	Spike frequency
1.0	2.5	4
2.0	1.2	10
3.0	0.8	20
4.0	0.6	30
5.0	0.5	40
6.0	0.45	50

* Parameters: x(0)=10.0; D=0.5

In summary, the spiked behavior of the lagged logistic model appears to be fairly robust with respect to the values of the parameters C, D and L. The spiked behavior is a general form of periodic instability in the model and not an idiosyncratic behavior dependent on the precise adjustment of parameter values. As noted in Schrodt (1981), the shape of the spikes and their timing can be further adjusted by using different values for the lag times [i is not equal to n in (1.2)] which introduces an additional degree of freedom into the model that may increase the possibility of fitting it to actual data.

RANDOM EFFECTS

Equation (2.1) gives a deterministic model of the conflict process. While this is useful as a first approximation, any real-world conflict situation is likely to involve random elements. These take at least two forms:

a. Measurement error—randomness in the measurement of the level of conflict. This randomness is purely a function of the observation of the phenomenon and does not affect it directly.

b. Perturbations—random elements occurring outside the deterministic context of the system which affect the subsequent behavior of the system.

In the traditional linear model, the distinction between these two types of error is unimportant, since algebraically an error in the measurement of the variables

$$(Y + f) = a(X + e) + b \tag{3.1}$$

and perturbations

$$Y = aX + b + g \tag{3.2}$$

has the same effect, i.e., if $g = ae-f$, then (3.1) and (3.2) are identical.

In a dynamic system, on the other hand, the two types of random effects have different impacts. If the random effect is simply measurement error (*a*), then it affects the observed data at only one time point. In contrast, errors in the system itself—perturbations—are incorporated into the variable $x(t)$ itself and affects the subsequent performance of the system.

In the case of spiked behavior, measurement error is unlikely to be very important. Since the value of the variable at most points is zero, and the variable departs radically from zero at the spikes, minor measurement error of the type encountered in regression analysis is not likely to be a key concern of the investigator. World War II is hard to miss.

Perturbations, on the other hand, are likely to be very important both in estimation and in the real-world behavior of the model. The basic idea of the model is that current conflict levels are determined by past conflict levels. In a very simple model of the form of (2.1), it is obvious that not all possible sources of conflict can be incorporated into the model. Random acts of violence or cooperation not explicitly incorporated into the model can momentarily increase or decrease the level of conflict and this will be reflected in subsequent conflict behavior.

To use a classic example, Europe was clearly primed for war in 1914, but the timing of the assassination of the Archduke Ferdinand in Sarajevo 28 June 1914 could not be predicted. It is conceivable that World War I could have occurred in 1912 or 1916 had circumstances been different, but the war would have eventually occurred. Similarly, peasant revolts and urban riots can be set off—given appropriate preconditions —by hot weather, food shortages or minor acts of street violence. On the positive side, random events can temporarily decrease conflict and increase international cooperation. Environmental disasters tend to have this characteristic, as does successful conflict mediation by third parties. Since no model can incorporate all these features, they are left exogenous to the model as random perturbations.

When the random element is incorporated, the model has the form

$$dx/dt = x(t)*[C - D*x(t-L)] + e(t) \qquad (3.3)$$

where $e(t)$ is a random variable. I experimented with two forms of e:

Type I: $e(t) = 0$ for probability q
             $= M$ with probability (1-q)

Type II: $e(t)$ is Normal $(0,b)$

In the first instance, the error is zero for most values and on random occasions introduces a single change of magnitude M into the system. The parameter q was set quite small so that the occurrence of the change followed a Poisson distribution. In the Type II error a random element was added at each point in time but the magnitude was normally distributed with mean zero and variance b.[4]

Equation (3.3) was simulated using both types of error and two

110

general configurations: high error variances where the expected magnitude of the perturbation was around 5, and low errors where the expected magnitude was around 0.25. Both stable ($C = 1$, $L = 1$) and spiked ($C = 3$, $L = 1$) models were examined. In the study I looked primarily for qualitative rather than quantitative behaviors—figures 4 and 5 present samples of each system with multiple random trajectories overlaid on the deterministic trajectory (heavy line).

Generally there did not seem to be a great deal of difference in the behavior of the two types of error. In both cases, if the error variance became large (large q in Type I, large b in Type II), the behavior was virtually completely random, with the trajectories filling the entire space. The value of q appeared to be more important than the value of M in the Type I perturbation. In both cases, the perturbations had relatively little effect in the initial stages of the model (i.e., the stages where it had not settled down to either an equilibrium or zero/spike behavior) and were more noticeable in the later stages.

Figure 4 gives an example of the behavior of a stable system. The trajectory is not surprising—the trajectories deviate occasionally from the equilibrium but then settle back to it again. There is no particular pattern to the deviations of the trajectories.

The situation becomes more interesting in the spiked case, as illustrated in figure 5. The random perturbations induce additional spikes, as expected. Unexpectedly, these random spikes appear to cluster themselves in a nonrandom fashion. This situation occurs when the random perturbations are relatively rare (Type I) or small (Type II), but occur under both Type I and II error conditions. In the Type II error situation, the frequency of the induced spikes is almost exactly twice the frequency of the deterministic spikes. The clustering of the spikes seems to be nonrandom, and it is not due to the apparent clustering seen in Poisson events; truly random spikes are produced at high levels of perturbations and these look quite different from the periodic spikes of the low-level perturbations.

While I have not explored the mathematical explanation for this in depth, I suspect this phenomenon occurs for the following reason. When the model is producing a spike deterministically, the additional perturbation has some effect on the magnitude of the spike but does not substantially change its shape. After the spike has peaked, the lagged effect of the spike creates a "shadow" in the period of time following the spike where perturbations are rapidly dampened out by the lagged

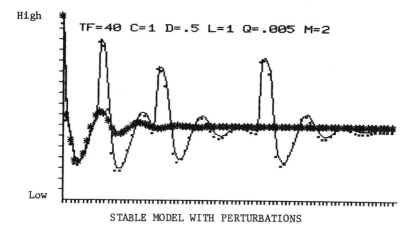

STABLE MODEL WITH PERTURBATIONS

Figure 4

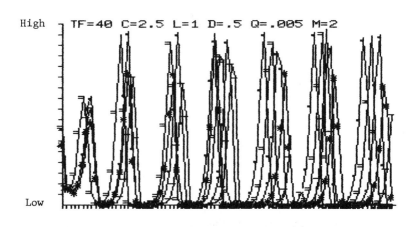

Figure 5

effect of the spike. When this shadow ends, the perturbations once again induce spikes into what would otherwise be the zero-level condition of the equation. The length of the shadow is a function of the perturbation size and it appears that the shadow is roughly one-half the length of the deterministic frequency of the spikes. The precise timing of induced spikes is, of course, randomly produced but in general a model containing a random element would have spikes at roughly twice the frequency of the deterministic model.

This result is interesting in two respects. First, the apparent existence of a temporal shadow in the wake of a spike corresponds to the observed characteristic that major levels of conflict are usually followed by periods of relative peace. This is a normal condition—conflict results in a great deal of death and destruction which cannot be repeated incessantly without intervals of peace—but it is interesting that this feature is incorporated into the model without any additional assumptions. Second, the addition of perturbations does not qualitatively change the behavior of the spiked model—it still produced spiked behavior. Only the frequency changed.

There is one other possible type of random behavior which might occur in the model, but which I've been unable to trigger thus far. Winfree (1980) discusses conditions under which a perturbation with proper timing and magnitude can cause a periodic system to degenerate into behavior which appears chaotic. For example, an optimally mistimed mild electrical shock to the heart can change the regular heartbeat to a chaotic and fatal filibration. The system discussed here may have this property, though if it does the effect is subtle. I have experimented triggering Type I errors of various magnitudes at each of 100 regularly-spaced points between spikes and was unable to induce the chaotic behavior, but this was a crude test and more detailed analysis might determine the proper timing and magnitude.

The attractiveness of the chaotic behavior is that it could serve as a model for systems which degenerate from periodic conflict to periods of almost continuous unpredictable conflict. Lebanon after 1976, Cambodia/Kampuchea after 1970, China 1920-1950 (and perhaps 1965-1970), Mexico 1910-1920 are examples of this type of long-term chaotic conflict. It is possible that chaos could be induced even in a system where the perturbation had to be precisely timed, since political actors interested in disrupting the system would have some idea (intuitively, rather than through formal models) of when the system was at a point in its cycle when the shock would be effective. The chaos would continue until external or internal factors in the system had changed to the extent that the original model was no longer applicable.

PROSPECTS FOR AN EMPIRICAL TEST

The persistence of the spiked behavior across a wide range of parameter values in the deterministic model and across the addition of random perturbations in the stochastic model suggest that an empirical fit of the model should be possible.

An informal attempt at this is shown in figure 6, where the model is fitted to the European dyadic war data and—without attempting any formal measures—the fit "looks" good. The model in this instance was fitted by hand using a lag of $L = 1.5$ and manipulation of the C and D parameters. In general the timing of the spikes is relatively accurate, with the major error being the World War I spike occurring about ten years too early. By setting $C = 2.0$, the model will predict WWI correctly but predict WWII about ten years too late, so the model is inaccurate in predicting the length of the inter-war period. The magnitude of the first two spikes is overestimated, but the magnitude of the second two spikes is approximately correct; the relative magnitude of the first two spikes is also correctly modeled. Figure 6 is not meant to be a conclusive test of the model, and might be improved with systematic curve-fitting methods. But it does indicate that there is some correspondence between the observed and predicted behavior.

A quantitative measure of the fit is more difficult. Because the data consist of very small and very large values, with little in between, a conventional squared error measure is likely to indicate that the model fits

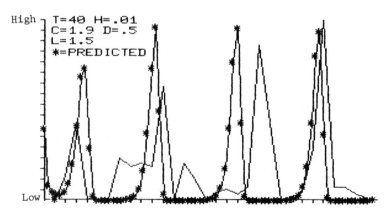

Empirical fit of lagged logistic model to European dyadic war data

Figure 6

poorly if the timing is even slightly off. In particular, the squared error for a predicted spike which misses an observed spike by a small amount will be just as great as that of a spike which misses by a large amount. Nonetheless, the former situation is clearly preferable to the latter since it gives a more accurate timing for the spike, which is the key variable of interest.

It might further be argued that if one accepts that perturbations (as opposed to simple measurement error) occur in the real world, then it is unrealistic to assume that highly accurate predictions will be possible, though at the same time it is possible to achieve a level of accuracy greater than that expected by chance. The problem of measuring the degree of fit, therefore, becomes one of measuring the temporal accuracy of the spikes without worrying too much about the magnitudes (except perhaps in the early stages of the model).

I would suggest two possible ways to do this measurement, one based on the intuitive appearance of the model and one based on the random structure.

The first model would measure the difference between the timing of the spikes. This would require a more precise definition of "spike" —which would not be difficult in most spiked data—and then measuring the mean difference between the observed spike and the nearest predicted spike. One might also include a separate measure for spike magnitude. If a measure could be established, the model could presumably be fitted using numerical function minimization (Schrodt, Gillespie and Zinnes, 1978) on the three parameters C, D, and L or possibly on the six parameters g, h, i, n, I and N of the original model (1.2). From a practical standpoint, this is the most useful measure, since it gives the expected error in the prediction of timing and would distinguish data which follow the predictions closely from those which are generally random. It ignores, however, any explicit consideration of the perturbations.

A second measure would fit perturbations into the model to induce spikes where necessary. The object of this measure would be to minimize the number of added perturbations necessary to bring the predictions of the model within a certain range of error. The statistical test would compare the predictions of the model against those of a null, random model—perhaps Poisson—of spikedness which had the same statistical characteristics as the observed data. This approach provides an explicit mechanism for incorporating the fact that perturbations exist in the real world and affect timing.

If a measure could be established, there are a number of candidates for empirical tests. A crude (hand-fitted) test of the European international conflict system has already been presented. The Japanese peasant revolts—or probably peasant revolts in any feudal system—is another possibility, as illustrated in figure 2. The apparent 20-year cycle of revolutionary activity and civil disturbance in Paris during the period 1790-1980 clearly invites a model such as this. The continued warfare in the Middle East—the study of which originally inspired this model—is another candidate. As long as the timing of the spikes is the key issue, there are relatively few measurement problems. By definition, spikes involve large-scale conflict whose existence is rarely in question; while the exact magnitudes of conflict spike may be uncertain, their timing is usually known precisely. The model is clearly testable, but a statistically meaningful measure must be established first.

CONCLUSION

International behavior is frequently characterized by rapid increases and decreases in the level of violence, and ideally this characteristic should be incorporated into models of international behavior. To date, models of behavior are incapable of modeling sudden changes (e.g., Richardson model), can predict the onset of conflict but not its termination (e.g., J-curve in domestic conflict), or have generated the complex behavior through complex models (e.g., most simulations). The lagged logistic model is a simple formulation which produces the spiked behavior by using a single equation and a small number of parameters.

The behavior exhibited by this model also suggests an interesting question with respect to system breakdown. Is the system breaking down, or is the system merely exhibiting behavior generated by its own dynamics (with or without random perturbations) which we did not expect? As noted in the introduction, with few exceptions the actors involved in the system do not change across the boundary between peace and war. A model that does not require a change in the dynamics of the system in order to generate the sudden increase in conflict is more plausible than a model which requires some sort of change.

The lagged logistic model is probably only one of a number of parsimonious models which produce spiked behavior. Furthermore, it may be the correct model for the wrong reasons: the "nationalist/internationalist" scheme I have outlined is plausible but does not uniquely determine the equation. Other mechanisms might produce similar behavior. The important point is that there is at least one model which can produce both protracted and periodic conflict with modifications of a single parameter and which is robust with respect to stochastic perturbations.

Of course, the whole of human striving and suffering, the heroism of revolution and the horror of massacre, the grand sweep of cultural, political, economic and technological change cannot be reduced to a single lagged logistic equation. The equation is only a guide to what *can* happen, not what *must* happen; it is important for what it suggests rather than for what it may or may not precisely predict. It is possible that the mechanisms underlying elements of social behavior over time may be simpler than we imagined, and that sudden change in that system may be a part of its natural dynamic.

NOTES

1. Simulation was done on an Apple II computer in Pascal. Pascal's real-number accuracy is 24 binary bits, or around 8 decimal digits. For large values of C round-off error bombs out of the simulation. The values near zero are very, very small—on the order of 10^{-25}—which is probably a bit small for real political purposes though it might, in pragmatic terms, represent the size of isolated cells of dissidents.

2. Euler's method is relatively inefficient but reliable—I experimented with a Runge-Kutta method but got very weird results. If there is a better method of approximating difference-differential equations I would appreciate hearing about it.

Because Euler's method is only an approximation and one using difference equations at that, it is conceivable that a purely differential model would not display the spiked behavior. Differencing intervals down to 0.001 were used with the spiked behavior still occurring, so if the phenomenon disappears at some point the differencing intervals must be extremely small.

3. The "$^\frown$" indicates exponentiation—i.e., 10^{12} is 10 to the 12th power.

4. The use of a normally-distributed error leads to the possibility that $x(t)$ will become negative. As indicated in Schrodt (1981), the result of $x(t) < 0$ would be an exponential decrease of x to minus infinity. Several people have observed that negative values of x violate some of the original reasons for formulating the model and, on further consideration, I think they are right. Thus when experimenting with Type II errors I "filtered" negative values of $x(t)$ by either (*a*) ignoring them and setting $x(t) = x(t-h)$ when $x(t) < 0$ or (*b*) setting $x(t) = |x(t)|$, which was used to correct negative values which appeared to be occuring due to round-off error. Both corrections are somewhat *ad hoc* but do not seem to have a major effect on the behavior of the model (though they were occasionally invoked), since similar behavior was observed with the Type I error, which does not have this problem.

REFERENCES

Azar, Edward E., and Cohen, Stephen. 1979. Peace as Crisis and War as Status-Quo: The Arab-Israeli Conflict Environment. *International Interactions* 6:2, pp. 159-84.

Azar, Edward E.; Jureidini, Paul; and McLaurin, Robert. 1978. Protracted Social Conflict: Theory and Practice in the Middle East. *Journal of Palestinian Studies* 8:1 pp. 41-60.

Borton, Hugh. 1968. *Peasant Uprisings in Japan of the Tokugawa Period.* (Second Edition). New York: Paragon Reprint Book Corporation.

Davis, William W.; Duncan, George; and Siverson, Randolph M. 1978. The Dynamics of Warfare, 1816-1965. *American Journal of Political Science* 22:4, pp. 772-92.

Hale, Jack. 1971. *Functional Differential Equations.* New York: Springer-Verlag.

Huckfeldt, R. Robert; Kohfeld, C. W.; and Likens, Thomas W. 1982. *Dynamic Modeling: An Introduction.* Beverly Hills: Sage.

May, Robert A. 1976. Simple Mathematical Models with Very Complicated Dynamics. *Nature* 261, pp. 459-67.

Olnick, Michael. 1978. *An Introduction to Mathematical Models in the Social and Life Sciences.* Reading, Mass.: Addison:Wesley.

Ross, Shepley. 1964. *Differential Equations.* Waltham, Mass.: Blaisdell Publishing.

Schrodt, Philip A. 1981. A Mathematical Model of the Persistence of Conflict. *International Interactions* 8:4, pp. 335-48.

Schrodt, Philip A.; Gillespie, John V.; and Zinnes, Dina A. 1978. Parameter Estimation by Numerical Minimization Methods. *International Interactions* 4:3, pp. 279-301.

Winfree, Arthur T. 1980. *The Geometry of Biological Time.* New York: Springer-Verlag.

6

AN EVENT MODEL OF CONFLICT INTERACTION

Dina A. Zinnes

Wars and international crises have often been viewed as system or subsystem breakdowns. When the multifaceted relations between a set of nations polarizes into conflict, the prior structure of communication and interaction between the protagonists has been destroyed. Cioffi's framework allows one to estimate the overall reliability of a system and thus predict a system's propensity for collapse. This chapter takes a deterministic approach to the same problem. Specifically, the goal is to develop a model capable of predicting system breakdown, i.e., crisis and war.

International crises and wars are almost invariably the end product of a sequence of events. Two nations do not typically go to war unless there has been a prior series of actions and reactions. Surprisingly, however, few researchers have studied crisis and war from this perspective. Although there have been analyses of hostile action-reaction patterns (Wilkenfeld, et al., 1972; Burrowes and Garriago-Pico, 1974; Azar, et al., 1974), there have been almost no studies of the relationship of these patterns to crisis and war. Yet the action-reaction patterns that precede a crisis or war undoubtedly contain clues of the impending system breakdown. Is it possible to develop a model of precrisis activity that can predict crisis and war? This was the goal of the Zinnes, et al. (1982) study. Using three variations of the Richardson action-reaction model, the study proposed that precrisis periods should evidence patterns of instability, i.e., the pattern of hostile interaction should

---

*Support for this research was granted by the Defense Advanced Research Project Agency, Office of Army Research, under Contract MDA-903-80-C-0149. The author thanks Michael Tennefoss for his aid in conducting the analyses and Barbara Hill for her efforts in compiling the tables.

escalate to such an extent that it would be possible to observe a "blow-up" of activity. By fitting Richardson-type models to the events that preceded international crises, it could be determined whether periods prior to major crises or wars were characterized by an unstable hostility pattern. Empirical tests on fourteen different post-World War II crises produced two surprising results. First, the empirical tests of the models suggested that nations in precrisis periods did not interact, i.e., one nation's behavior was not clearly a consequence of the other's previous activities. Second, precrisis periods were *not* characterized by instability.

The Zinnes, et al. study, however, followed in the mold of previous empirical analyses of conflict interaction. Thus like Wilkenfeld, et al. (1972); Burrowes and Garriago-Pico (1974); and Azar, et al. (1974), the Zinnes, et al. study adopted a "tennis match" approach to conflict interaction and assumed that the variable of interest was so much activity *per time unit*. The tennis match approach looks first at X, then at Y, then back at X, etc. Thus the historical sequence of events is lost. If X initiates three events before Y responds, then the sequence of X's events is lost by looking back and forth between X and Y. In periods prior to a major crisis or war, this type of model could well obscure a very important underlying process. Suppose X initiates a small hostile act, but Y does nothing. X then initiates a stronger hostile act. Still no reaction. X then initiates a very hostile act. Now Y responds. The buildup in hostility that has occurred across the successive hostile acts is lost by looking first at X, then at Y, then back at X, etc.

The second characteristic of "stimulus-response" or action-reaction studies is the assumption that the relevant variable is activity *per time unit*. Time is used as a metric or scale against which activity is measured. Hence, the number or intensity of X's acts toward Y is determined by some arbitrary unit like a day or a week, e.g., so many hostile acts or so much hostile activity per day. Such an approach assumes that the "ruler," i.e., the unit of time used, is unchanging. Pierre Allan (1980) has argued, however, that this assumption is unwarranted. Particularly in periods of crisis, decision makers operate in terms of a very different time scale ("diplomatic time"), a time scale that is not a simple linear function of real time but a complicated function of the unfolding events. Furthermore, using time as a ruler against which activity is measured does not allow one to assess how time itself affects and is affected by the interactive activity. Durations between hostile events have an impact on the intensity of subsequent hostile events.

It is reasonable, then, to question whether the unusual results obtained in the Zinnes, et al. (1982) study might not be a matter of inappropriate assumptions. A more realistic model of hostile interaction might produce the results originally anticipated. Thus it would seem that to study the dynamic, explosive buildup of activity that produces a system or subsystem breakdown, the models need to be revised and refocused. Such revisions should: (1) capture the buildup in activity across the entire system, (2) eliminate the arbitrary time scale, and (3) permit time to function as a variable. In the following pages, a model will be developed which focuses not on time, or so much activity per time unit, but on the occurrence of an event. The model describes how attributes of events, their intensity and the duration between them, interact. The closing sections report a series of empirical tests and a slightly revised version of the model.

AN EVENT BASED MODEL OF PRECRISIS BEHAVIOR

Since the focus of this study is on precrisis behavior, the central variable of interest is hostility. The goal is to develop a model of hostile interaction based not on arbitrary time units like days or weeks, but on the actual occurrence of hostile events. This is not to say that time does not play a role in the new model. Precrisis activities are still considered as an evolving process and the occurrence of hostile events is still seen in a time-ordered sequence. However, in the new model the independent variable of the process is no longer time but the *event*. Instead of defining hostility with respect to units of time, e.g., $x(t)$ as the amount of hostility emitted by X to Y on a given day or during a week, we will now talk in terms of $h(i)$, the hostile intensity of the ith event. To clarify this conceptualization, we define:

event set i: the totality of hostile events that occur within a specified time interval.

It would be ideal if every event were recorded by the exact time at which it occurred. This would make possible a precise time ordering, or chronology, of events. Unfortunately, this is not possible. Events recorded in public sources like newspapers are typically recorded by day, at best. Consequently, it is not possible to think in terms of each ith event. One must instead consider an ith event set; namely, all events that occur within the span of time typically used by the recording instrument. This is normally a day or twenty-four hours. Given three events in a single 24-hour period, all three must be thought of as composing an event set.

The symbol i is an index which runs from 1, the first event set in a sequence, to n, the last event set in the series. It is important to emphasize that the index i only specifies the position of a specific event set within the context of a series. Since event sets are not an explicit function of time, there is no way of knowing when, in terms of real time, event set 8, for example, occurred.

We next define several functions based on the event set i. Let:

$d(i)$ = the time that elapses between event set i and event set $(i + 1)$.

"Time" could be measured in any metric, but, given the nature of event data sets, the most useful scale is days. Thus

$d(3) = 6$

would indicate that the amount of time between the third event set and the fourth event set was six days. These two definitions provide the basis for beginning the construction of the model. An argument frequently found in the crisis literature suggests that as the crisis approaches, there is less and less time between events; events occur in increasingly rapid succession. The amount of time available for planning and thinking through possible responses is thus longer in the earlier phases of the interaction sequence and decreases as the crisis approaches. One mathematical representation of this statement would be:

$$d(i + 1) - d(i) = a_1 d(i) \qquad (1)$$

This statement actually says something more specific than is found in the literature. Equation (1) says that changes in the durations between successive event sets is a function of the length of time between the previous event sets. The literature only indicates that the time intervals are getting shorter; it does not explain *why* these durations are shrinking. Equation (1) proposes that the changes are a function of the previous duration. Furthermore, equation (1) is more general than the previous statements, since a_1 can be either positive or negative. However, the crisis literature is proposing:

$a_1 < 0.$

Since $d(i)$ is always a positive number,
$a_1 < 0 \longrightarrow \quad d(i + 1) - d(i) < 0 \longrightarrow \quad d(i + 1) < d(i),$
i.e., each successive duration is smaller.

A graphical representation of equation (1) is given in figure 1:

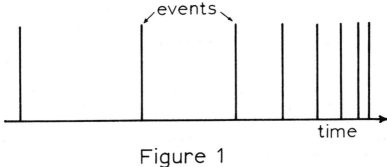

Figure 1

But equation (1) does not adequately represent a relationship implicit in the crisis literature. One could interpret the crisis literature as arguing that the durations between succeeding events is decreasing as a function of the hostility of the events. To capture this ingredient in the model, another definition is needed:

$h(i)$ = the intensity of hostility of event set i. Equation (1) can now be modified to state:

$$d(i + 1) - d(i) = a_1 d(i) + a_2 h(i). \qquad (2)$$

Changes in durations between event sets are not only a function of the previous duration but, additionally, a function of the intensity of the previous hostile event set. To be in line with the literature, it is necessary to further postulate:

$$a_2 < 0,$$

since, if we look only at the impact of $h(i)$ on durations:

$$a_2 < \text{---} > d(i+1) - d(i) < 0 \text{---} > d(i+1) < d(i).$$

In other words, the level of hostility of the event set decreases the duration between the subsequent event sets. Note that any occurrence of a hostile event has this impact. However, a very hostile event will dramatically decrease the time until the next event, while a very mild hostile event, although still decreasing the next time interval, will only do so minimally. Note also that since it is assumed that both a_1 and a_2 are negative, both parameters work in the direction of making successive intervals smaller.

Although equation (2) appears to begin to capture several aspects of a precrisis process, a model which focuses only on durations between hostile event sets would not seem adequate. Consider, for example, figures 2 and 3 where the height of each bar reflects the intensity of an event set.

In both figures the durations between event sets are decreasing, yet neither would appear to be an appropriate representation of a precrisis period. Figure 2 would seem too random with respect to the intensity of the events, while figure 3 would seem to reflect a potential crisis that was actually defused. Figure 4 would appear to be a more appropriate representation of a precrisis period. The incorporation of $h(i)$ in equation (3) begins to capture the difference between figures 2 and 3 on the one hand, and figure 4 on the other. However, a more explicit statement is required to indicate how the intensities of hostility of subsequent event sets change.

As the sequence of events unfolds, bringing a pair of interacting nations closer to a crisis, it is reasonable to assume that the intensity of each succeeding hostile event is increasing. Indeed, it could be argued that, particularly in periods preceding war, changes in the intensity of the hostility of each succeeding event are a direct function of the intensity of the last event. This statement can be mathematically written as:

$$h(i+1) - h(i) = b_1 h(i). \tag{3}$$

However, to capture the dynamics shown in figure 4, it must be further specified that:

$$b_1 > 0,$$

since

$$b_1 > 0 \longrightarrow h(i+1) - h(i) > 0 \longrightarrow h(i+1) > h(i).$$

Each hostile event increases the intensity of the next hostile event.

But equation (3) is not sufficient. The argument that suggests that intensities affect durations can surely be reversed to say that durations

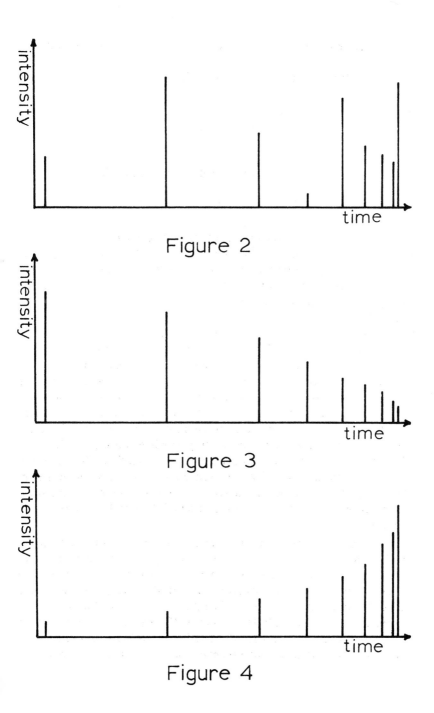

Figure 2

Figure 3

Figure 4

also affect intensities. We thus propose the following representation:

$$h(i+1) - h(i) = b_1 h(i) + b_2 d(i) \tag{4}$$

and assume

$$b_2 < 0,$$

since, looking only at the impact of duration on hostility:

$$b_2 < 0 \longrightarrow h(i+1) - h(i) < 0 \longrightarrow h(i+1) < h(i).$$

Thus the durations between the event sets will decrease the intensity of the succeeding event sets; durations provide a cooling down period. Although any duration between event sets will have the impact of making $h(i+1)$ less intense than $h(i)$, the longer the duration—i.e., the bigger $d(i)$—the less intense will the $h(i+1)$ event be in contrast to the $h(i)$ event.

Although we have analyzed the separate impacts of h and d on changes in h in equation (4), it must be noted that the two parameters, b_1 and b_2, are having simultaneous and *opposite* impacts on changes in h. Since the two parameters are working against each other, the ultimate final impact on h is unclear. This is in contrast to the situation with equation (2) where the two parameters worked in the same direction to decrease the intervals between successive event sets. Furthermore, the situation becomes more complex when considering the complete model, the composite of equations (2) and (4). Since the forces are operating simultaneously and in different directions, it is not clear how the variables h and d are ultimately affected. However, this question can be answered through a consideration of the stability properties of the model.

The stability properties of a dynamic model tell us something about the trajectories, $h(i)$ and $d(i)$. Specifically they indicate whether the intensity of hostility of successive event sets is growing in an unbounded and explosive fashion or whether it will settle down to come equilibrium value. If the system is unstable, then the former will be the case; if the system is stable, then the latter will occur. If the system is unstable, then this will mean that the intensity of hostility is growing without bounds and that the durations between event sets is becoming increasingly smaller at an explosive rate. If we combine equations (2) and (4):

$d(i+1) - d(i) = a_1 d(i) + a_2 h(i)$ and
$h(i+1) - h(i) = b_1 h(i) + b_2 d(i)$,

then the conditions for stability for a system of two difference equations are:

(a) $-(a_1 + b_1) < 4$
(b) $a_2 b_2 < (a_1 + 2)(b_1 + 2)$
(c) $a_2 b_2 < a_1 b_1$.

In order for a system of difference equations to be stable, all three conditions must be met. Consequently, if any one of the three conditions is not met, the system will be unstable. The assumptions that have been made on the signs of the parameters are not sufficient to check conditions *(a)* and *(b)*. They do, however, permit us to check condition *(c)*. Given:

$a_2 < 0$
$b_2 < 0$
$a_1 < 0$
$b_1 > 0$,

it is obvious that

$a_2 b_2 - a_1 b_1 > 0$,

which violates condition *(c)*. Given the assumptions on the signs of the parameters, the model will always be unstable. Consequently, if the model is an accurate picture of precrisis behavior, then it is capable of predicting system breakdown, i.e., crisis and war. If the equations together with the signs of the parameters are correct, then a clue to an impending crisis/war lies in the instability of the sequence of hostile acts.

Before discussing how this model might be tested, it is important to note a special characteristic of the model. This new "event-based" model considers only the *sequential ordering* of hostile event sets. There is nothing in the model to indicate who initiated the hostile event and who was the target. The model only considers a time-ordered sequence of event sets. The actors must therefore be introduced through the definition of the relevant event sets. There are clearly a variety of different ways to define the relevant event sets. For example:

actor-based model: the relevant event set is defined as those events initiated by a given actor X towards a specified actor Y

dyadic model: the relevant event set is defined as all events initiated by X towards Y and all events initiated by Y towards X.

While the implications of the actor-based model are probably obvious—only the events initiated by X toward Y are placed in the time-ordered sequence—the implications of the dyadic model may be less clear. Although the relevant event sets for the dyadic model include the directed dyadic interactions of X and Y, these event sets are put in a chronological sequence irrespective of initiator or target. It may be the case that actor X is responsible for event sets 1, 2 and 3 before actor Y initiates event set 4. For example, the data might appear as follows:

time	intensity of hostility		event set
(day)	X	Y	
1	3	0	1
2	0	0	—
3	5	0	2
4	6	0	3
5	0	2	4
6	7	5	5

Note that X initiated three events before Y responded, but that when these acts are translated into event sets they are simply placed in chronological order. Note further that since nothing occurred on day 2, no event set is defined. Finally, on day 6 both nations emit hostility toward one another, but since it is not possible to determine the time ordering of these occurrences, they are combined into a single event set.

Thus the event-based model, when applied to more than a single nation, is truly a "systemic" model of the total activity of the participating units. Although this is a very different way of thinking of action-reaction patterns, in many ways it is more realistic than the standard stimulus-response conceptualization. In the usual action-reaction model it is typically assumed that one nation's act causes another to respond, which in turn makes the first react, etc. But action-reaction can be more complex. A nation could begin by voicing a small grievance.

The other side says nothing. So the first nation makes a louder statement. Still no response. So the first nation sends a very strong statement. Now the second nation responds. While the addition of the events of two nations on a single day obscures the action-reaction pattern (since the model is looking at the course of events over both parties, from a systemic perspective), such fusion of event sets is justified.

The above two definitions of relevant event sets are only two of the more obvious applications of the event model. One could, for example, look at all events initiated by X with respect to a particular part of the world, or all events exchanged by a set of nations involved in a conflict situation. In short, the applicability of the model is very broad, and since the addition of participants only alters the definition of the relevant event sets and not the model (as would be the case in applying a Richardson type of model), such applications are relatively straightforward.

EVALUATING THE EVENTS BASED MODEL

To what extent do equations (2) and (4) capture the dynamics of successive event sets in periods prior to a crisis or war? To answer this question, three cases were selected for empirical tests. The six-month periods prior to the Arab-Israeli War of 1967 and the India-Pakistan War of 1971, and the 1973 U.S.-U.S.S.R. crisis in the Middle East. These three crises were chosen from a set of fourteen crisis cases that have been examined extensively using the more standard Richardson action-reaction model (Zinnes, et al., 1982). The three were chosen as a preliminary test and for the purposes of comparison with the earlier results. The data used to evaluate the event model were taken from the Conflict and Peace Data Bank (COPDAB) developed by Edward Azar.

The two equations of the model were each estimated separately, using first an actor-based definition of the relevant event sets and then using the dyadic definition of the relevant event sets. The results for equation (2),

$$d(i + 1) - d(i) = a_1 d(i) + a_2 h(i),$$

reported in table 1, are based on a multiple regression which might be diagrammed as shown in figure 5. Note that the hostile event whose intensity is affecting the changes in duration is the event which occurs before the first duration considered in the equation.

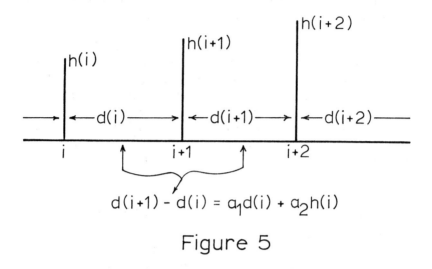

Figure 5

The adjusted r^2 values for the actor-based model are given in lines 1 and 2, 4 and 5, and 7 and 8. The results for the dyadic model are shown on lines 3, 6 and 9 and labeled as Both. As can be seen, the r^2 values are fairly high, indicating strong support for the model for both the actor-based and dyadic applications. Although the actor-based models provide strong support for the model in each of the three cases, the dyadic test produces a higher r^2 than for one of the actors.

Unfortunately, however, these results are marred by the results for the second parameter a_2. Not only is this parameter not statistically significant, it is also typically very small, i.e., close to zero, the exception being the USSR. Thus changes in duration appear to be largely a function of the previous duration. Note, however, that the parameter a_1 is negative, as postulated. Durations thus have a decreasing impact on subsequent durations.

TABLE 1

ESTIMATION RESULTS FOR DURATION EQUATION

Nation(s)	R2	Adjusted R2	Duration		Hostility	
			a1	s1	a2	s2
Arab states	.518	.508	-1.044	0	-0.002	.678
Israel	.386	.369	-0.718	0	0.008	.247
Both	.409	.397	-0.825	0	-0.001	.741
India	.535	.517	-1.077	.000	-0.014	.376
Pakistan	.447	.426	-0.904	.000	-0.007	.522
Both	.471	.458	-0.933	.000	-0.004	.184
U.S.	.676	.633	-1.197	.000	-0.016	.901
USSR	.368	.271	-0.711	.018	-0.403	.221
Both	.538	.504	-1.065	.000	-0.081	.339

NOTE: Estimated equation was:

$$d(i+1) - d(i) = a1\, d(i) + a2\, h(i)$$

131

Table 2 reports the results for the estimation of equation (4):

$$h(i+1) - h(i) = b_1 h(i) + b_2 d(i).$$

Although the adjusted r^2's for the Arabs and India do not provide strong support for the equation, the dyadic test produces r^2 values that indicate support for the equation in all three cases. A comparison of these results to findings on action-reaction analyses of hostility using Richardson-based models will follow.

A consideration of the parameters of equation (4), however, provides some surprising results. First, in contrast to equation (2) for the India-Pakistan case, both parameters b_1 and b_2 have an impact on the changes in hostility, i.e., neither of the parameters are close to zero. Unfortunately, however, the significance values of the b_2 parameter make it difficult to place much confidence in the impact of the duration variable. The second surprising result is the b_1 parameter. This parameter is statistically significant but without exception always negative. It will be recalled that it was assumed that this parameter would be positive. This suggests that the *changes* in the intensity of event sets is declining and that the intensity of *each subsequent event set* is declining. Had b_2 been positive but between 0 and 1, changes in hostility would have been declining but the actual intensity value of each subsequent event set would have been increasing.

We turn next to the stability analyses, reported in table 3. The first three columns give the stability results for equations (2) and (4), using the estimates of those equations given in tables 1 and 2. This table provides the alternate but equivalent analysis of stability (alternate from the earlier discussion) by reporting the eigenvalues. A system is stable *only* if the eigenvalues fall within the unit circle, i.e., the absolute value of both eigenvalues must be less than one. As is quickly seen, all cases are stable. It will be recalled that, given the assumptions placed on the signs of the parameters in the model, the model should have been unstable. Thus the stable results suggest that something has gone wrong with respect to the assumptions made about the parameter values. As we have just seen, the principal problem undoubtedly lies with the b_1 parameter. This parameter was assumed to be positive, but across all cases it is uniformly negative.

Although contrary to expectations, the model is uniformly stable across the three crises, and for both the actor-based and dyadic analyses, it is important to note that two interpretations of this result

TABLE 2

ESTIMATION RESULTS FOR HOSTILITY EQUATION

Nation(s)	R2	Adjusted R2	Hostility		Duration	
			b1	s1	b2	s2
Arab states	.306	.290	-0.604	0	0.509	.815
Israel	.606	.595	-1.182	0	2.047	.315
Both	.435	.424	-0.836	0	4.546	.368
India	.201	.170	-0.845	.001	-2.007	.343
Pakistan	.476	.456	-0.964	.000	-1.698	.345
Both	.416	.401	-0.828	.000	-3.962	.334
U.S.	.345	.257	-0.714	.017	-0.152	.759
USSR	.695	.648	-1.079	.000	-0.588	.006
Both	.395	.350	-0.774	.000	-0.321	.454

NOTE: Estimated equation was:

$$h(i+1) - h(i) = b1\ h(i) + b2\ d(i)$$

133

TABLE 3

STABILITY RESULTS FOR THE EVENT MODEL

Nation(s)	λ_1	λ_2	Stable or Unstable
Arab states	.394	-.042	S
Israel	.315	-.215	S
Both	.170 *	.170 *	S
India	.243	-.165	S
Pakistan	.179	-.047	S
Both	.256	-.017	S
U.S.	.291	-.202	S
USSR	.625	-.415	S
Both	.298	-.137	S

* Eigenvalues are complex numbers.
Only the real part is reported.

are possible. There are in effect two cases of stability (and two cases of instability) as shown in figure 6. It is clear from figure 6 that there are significantly different interpretations for each case. Although both stability cases show the variable h(i) moving towards the equilibrium value of the system, the h(i) trajectory above the equilibrium line shows this trajectory coming *down* into the equilibrium value. This indicates that each successive ith event is *decreasing in intensity*. The h(i) trajectory below the equilibrium line, however, shows that each successive ith event is *increasing* in intensity. If the system is stable, then one would certainly anticipate that the h(i) trajectory in precrisis periods would belong in the second of the two stability cases. The intensity of hostility should be *increasing* from event to event. If the system is moving to an equilibrium, that equilibrium value should represent an intense level of hostility.

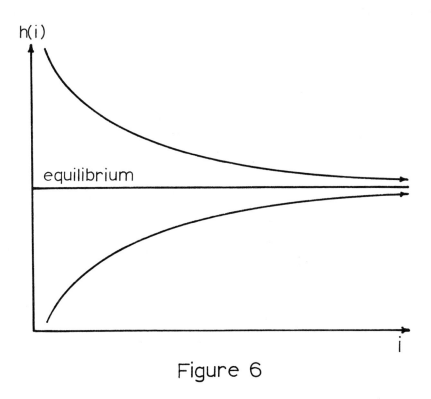

Figure 6

Testing for the correct stability interpretation requires that the equilibrium point of the system be found. This is accomplished by setting equations (2) and (4) equal to zero and then solving for $h(i)$ and $d(i)$. A comparison of the initial value of the $h(i)$ trajectory (i.e., the intensity value of the first hostile event in the series), and the hostility equilibrium value determines the correct stability case. If the initial condition value is larger than the equilibrium value, then it is stability case one; if the initial condition value is smaller than the equilibrium value, then it is stability case two. These results are found in the last three columns of table 4. With the exception of the USSR, the hostility trajectory is stable in the case two sense, i.e., the initial conditions are smaller than the $h(i)$ equilibrium value. Thus while the system is *not* explosive as had been expected, it is stable in the case two sense. This then provides a different explanation for the crisis event: the dynamics of the process are *forcing* the intensity of each subsequent hostile event to be larger as the $h(i)$ trajectory moves towards the equilibrium value. Perhaps the equilibrium value represents that amount of hostility at which the crisis occurs.

But while one would expect the $h(i)$ trajectory to be stable in the case two sense, one would anticipate the $d(i)$ trajectory to be stable in the case one sense. Early in the crisis the durations between events should be long, but as the crisis approaches, the durations should become shorter. The initial value for the $d(i)$ trajectory should be larger than the equilibrium value for $d(i)$. These results are found in the first three columns of table 4. The results here are mixed. In the India-Pakistan case two of the tests (India and Both) do not support the prediction; in the U.S.-USSR case the USSR test does not support the prediction.

A COMPARISON OF THE EVENT MODEL
AND ACTION-REACTION MODELS

Since the three cases used to evaluate the event model have been estimated by using more standard action-reaction models, a comparison of results across models is of interest. Before such a comparison is made, however, it is important to note the types of models employed in earlier studies and the differences between those models and the event model that has been proposed and tested here. In an earlier study (Zinnes, et al., 1982) three basic models were examined.

TABLE 4

EQUILIBRIUM RESULTS FOR THE EVENT MODEL

Nation(s)	DURATION			HOSTILITY		
	Initial Value	Equilibrium Value	Slope*	Initial Value	Equilibrium Value	Slope*
Arab states	1	0.925	F	16	58.430	R
Israel	5	1.316	F	16	48.568	R
Both	1	0.632	F	16	84.388	R
India	1	2.048	R	6	39.141	R
Pakistan	5	2.052	F	16	47.462	R
Both	0	1.153	R	6	57.990	R
U.S.	24	6.898	F	6	16.473	R
USSR	7	8.857	R	16	14.742	F
Both	7	4.512	F	16	17.651	R

* F: falling (decreasing) slope
   R: rising (increasing) slope

These can be mathematically represented as follows:

Model 1:
$$x(t+1) - x(t) = a_1 x(t)$$
$$y(t+1) - y(t) = b_1 y(t)$$

Model 2:
$$x(t+1) - x(t) = a_2 y(t)$$
$$y(t+1) - y(t) = b_2 x(t)$$

Model 3:
$$x(t+1) - x(t) = a_1 x(t) + a_2 y(t)$$
$$y(t+1) - y(t) = b_1 y(t) + b_2 x(t)$$

where $x(t)$ are the hostile acts initiated by X towards Y over some specified time interval t, and $y(t)$ has a similar interpretation. As can be seen, model 1 is a noninteractive autoregressive model. Model 2 is the directed interaction model, and model 3 is a combination of models 1 and 2. Each of these three models has been estimated using two different data sets, WEIS and COPDAB. The WEIS data set only provides frequencies, so the variables $x(t)$ and $y(t)$ are measured by the number of hostile acts that one nation directs towards another over a given time interval. When the WEIS data were used, the data were aggregated over ten-day periods. The COPDAB data set provides not only the frequency of directed hostile events between pairs of nations, but also provides the intensities of those events. Thus when using the COPDAB data set it was possible to run two sets of analyses—one using only frequencies (as a comparison with the WEIS analyses), and one using the intensity values. The data were not aggregated and the analyses were done over days.

If we compare the above three models with the event model, it becomes immediately obvious that the only appropriate comparison is with the hostility equation in the event model. Since models 1, 2 and 3 do not contain any variable comparable to the duration equation:

$$d(i+1) - d(i) = a_1 d(i) + a_2 h(i),$$

it makes little sense to contrast the results for this equation with those obtained for models 1, 2 or 3. The hostility equation, however, does provide a basis for comparison:

$$h(i+1) - h(i) = b_1 h(i) + b_2 d(i).$$

Although the hostility equation and models 1, 2 and 3 are all based on the directed hostility between two nations, the hostility equation differs from models 1, 2 and 3 in that it contains a new variable—duration. A comparison between the hostility equation and models 1, 2 and 3 is thus an examination of the relative value of this new parameter.

Meaningful comparisons, however, require that careful attention be paid to the appropriate comparisons. Since model 1 is a simple autoregressive system which does not consider the behavior of the other nation, the appropriate comparison for model 1 in the event model is the actor-based analysis of the hostility equation. Although both models 2 and 3 contain interaction, model 3 contains both an autoregressive component and an interactive component. Thus model 3 would appear to be the better comparison for the dyadic test of the hostility equation. Although it is of interest to compare all three analyses of models 1 and 3—WEIS-based frequency analyses, COPDAB-based frequency and COPDAB-based intensity analyses—the most appropriate comparison is between the intensity values of the COPDAB data set. This is because the hostility equation of the event model is a direct function of the intensity of hostile events.

The comparative results are provided in table 5. The first two columns are the multiple and adjusted multiple r^2 for the event model as reported in table 2. Columns 3 and 4 give the results for models 1 and 3 using WEIS data. The results for the COPDAB data are given in columns 5 through 8. The U.S.-USSR case was analyzed in the WEIS data in two separate periods—1970 and 1973. Thus, as can be seen in table 5, there are two WEIS comparisons to be made with the single event model analysis. Boxes have been placed around the results that are most comparable according to the above discussion. Although the event model generally does appreciably better than the WEIS estimates, there does not appear to be much difference between the event model on the one hand and the intensity version of COPDAB on the other. The fact that the event model makes no real improvement over COPDAB's intensity results further confirms, in both models 1 and 3 and the actor-based and dyadic versions of the event model, the primary importance of the intensity of hostility in precrisis periods. The incorporation of the duration variable has not taken us much beyond the simple action-reaction model.

There is a further comparison that is of interest. One of the surprising results obtained in fitting the hostility equation was the fact that the b_1 parameter—the parameter modifying hostility—was negative and

TABLE 5

A COMPARISON OF EVENT MODEL AND ACTION-REACTION MODELS

Nation(s)	Event Model		WEIS		COPDAB			
			Model 1	Model 3	Model 1		Model 3	
					F	I	F	I
Arab states	.306	.290*	-.062	.162*	.17	.22	.17*	.25*
Israel	.606	.595**	.182	.141*	.37	.48	.40*	.49**
Both	.435	.401*						
India	.201	.170*	-.055	.024*	.40	.39	.42*	.45*
Pakistan	.476	.456**	.017	.334**	.32	.33	.32*	.33**
Both	.416	.401*						
U.S.	.345	.257**	.185	.127*	.48	.45	.51*	.43*
USSR	.695	.648**	.410	.558*	.49	.42	.48*	.45**
Both	.395	.350*						

* Adjusted R2

140

not positive. A similar finding occurs for the COPDAB intensity estimates for model 1: the a_1 parameter is negative. While this similarity is somewhat to be expected, it must be pointed out that there is an important difference between model 1 and the hostility equation. The estimation of model 1 in the COPDAB data involved the correlation of X's hostility toward Y from day to day, including days on which no hostility was in evidence. The estimation of the hostility equation was a correlation over successive events. In any case, from both perspectives, changes in the intensity of hostility decline as a function of the intensity of the previous event.

Finally it should be noted that for each of the analyses of models 1 and 3 reported in table 5, stability analyses were conducted. In all cases the models were found to be stable. Thus the results for the event model again parallel those for the action-reaction model.

CONSTRUCTING A MODIFIED EVENT MODEL

A defect of the event model is its sole reliance on hostility. While hostile events are clearly germane to the onset of a crisis, it is also the case that precrisis periods often see cooperative activity. As nations become concerned over the implications of hostile interactions, attempts are made to resolve the areas of contention. It would seem important, then, to incorporate cooperative acts into the model. There are a variety of ways this might be done, but for the explorative purposes of the present analysis, we will propose only one approach. The focus will remain on hostility, and cooperative events will enter the model in relationship to the occurrence of hostile event sets. We therefore define:

event set i' = all cooperative events that occur between hostile event set i and hostile event set $(i + 1)$.

The definition of a cooperative event set differs from the definition of a hostile event set in three significant ways. First, a cooperative event set is defined in relationship to hostile event sets. Thus cooperative event set 2, by definition, falls between hostile event sets 2 and 3. Second, because a cooperative event set is defined in relationship to a pair of hostile event sets, the cooperative event set i' must be the sum of all cooperative events that take place between the two hostile event sets. Unlike hostile event sets, the chronology of cooperative event sets is somewhat collapsed. This means that while hostile event sets are defined in terms of a constant time frame, 24 hours, cooperative event sets cover variable time frames. Third, unlike hostile event sets, cooperative event sets can be empty, i.e., zero; it is not necessary that cooperative events occur between any successive hostile event sets. Let:

f(i') = the intensity of cooperation of event set i'.

Since cooperative event sets are sums of cooperative events occurring in intervals between hostile event sets, the intensity of the event set i' will be the sum of the intensities of the cooperative events. We can now modify equations (2) and (4) by adding this new variable:

$$d(i+1) - d(i) = a_1 d(i) + a_2 h(i) + a_3 f(i') \tag{5}$$
$$h(i+1) - h(i) = b_1 h(i) + b_2 d(i) + b_3 f(i'). \tag{6}$$

The following analysis:

$$a_3 > 0 \longrightarrow d(i+1) - d(i) > 0 \longrightarrow d(i+1) > d(i)$$
$$b_3 < 0 \longrightarrow h(i+1) - h(i) < 0 \longrightarrow h(i+1) < h(i)$$

indicates that the most reasonable assumption on the new parameters is to propose that cooperative activities increase durations and decrease the intensity of hostility. As was true in the case of the original event model, this modified model can be applied to a single actor, or to two or more actors.

Using the same cases and data sets, the estimates for equations (5) and (6) are given in tables 6 and 7. A comparison of table 6 for the duration equation and table 1 indicates essentially no change in the r^2 values. In addition, the hostility variable continues to have basically no impact on changes in duration. The duration variable has the greatest impact on equation (5). The cooperative variable, like hostility, appears to have very little impact. When the parameter value for this variable is statistically significant (the Israeli, USSR and U.S.-USSR Both cases), it is typically very small. Comparing table 7 with table 2 again shows that the correlations are basically unaffected by the inclusion of the cooperative variable. Furthermore, hostility continues to be the significant component of the estimation, both in terms of size and significance levels, and it continues to be negative. Both duration and cooperation appear to have an impact on hostility in the Arab-Israeli and India-Pakistan cases (the values of these parameters are not zero), but the poor significance levels of these parameters do not permit us to place much weight on these findings. Although the significance of the parameter weights does not permit clear conclusions, it is of interest to note that the sign of the cooperation parameter is as predicted, with the exception of the Israeli and Pakistan cases.

CONCLUSION

The results from the three cases indicate that the event-based model does provide a reasonable interpretation of precrisis activity, for both single actors and dyads. At least, insofar as the event model proposes that durations affect subsequent durations and the intensity of hostile event sets affect the intensity of subsequent event sets, the analyses suggest that this new interpretation has some merit. But, while these results support the new interpretation of precrisis activity, this support is mixed. Durations affect subsequent durations, yet the intensity of the hostile event that precedes the durations does not directly affect the change in durations. It is important to consider the appropriate interpretation of this result. Hostility does affect durations because the durations are being measured with respect to the occurrence of a hostile event set. Thus the fact that previous durations affect subsequent durations is information about the relationship between hostile event sets. The analysis of the duration equation then indicates that it is the time relationship between event sets that is of importance, and that this time relationship is not influenced by the intensity of hostility of an event set. It is the occurrence of the hostile event rather than its intensity that influences the subsequent occurrence of hostile events.

But the intensity of hostility is not irrelevant to precrisis behavior. The analysis of the hostility equation clearly shows that the intensity of previous hostile events has a direct bearing on the intensity of subsequent hostile events. But the surprising result is that the intensities are decreasing. The fact that previous analyses of action-reaction models provide very similar results strengthens the importance of this finding but does not help to supply any explanation. Unfortunately it is unclear whether durations affect changes in the intensity of hostility, given the high p values for the parameters of the duration variable.

Although the results for the hostility equation are not appreciably different from the r^2 values obtained through analyses of standard action-reaction models, the fact that the event model does at least as well and sometimes better than the action-reaction model (together with the new information provided by the duration equation) is sufficient basis for continuing work on the events model. The issue, however, is whether the best or most appropriate event model has been considered. Is it really true that the intensity of a hostile event has no effect on the

TABLE 6

ESTIMATION RESULTS FOR MODIFIED DURATION EQUATION

Nation(s)	R2	Adjusted R2	Duration		Hostility		Cooperation	
			a1	s1	a2	s2	a3	s3
Arab states	.519	.502	-1.053	.000	-0.002	.677	0.008	.802
Israel	.414	.389	-0.825	.000	0.008	.235	0.029	.073
Both	.409	.391	-0.829	.000	-0.001	.739	0.000	.957
India	.542	.515	-1.073	0	-0.015	.354	-0.090	.381
Pakistan	.447	.415	-0.906	0	-0.007	.529	0.028	.874
Both	.479	.458	-0.942	0	-0.004	.155	-0.061	.299
U.S.	.719	.659	-1.686	.001	-0.052	.680	0.094	.164
USSR	.593	.492	-1.222	.001	-0.235	.400	0.159	.024
Both	.663	.624	-1.650	.000	-0.071	.337	0.078	.005

TABLE 7

ESTIMATION RESULTS FOR MODIFIED HOSTILITY EQUATION

Nation(s)	R2	Adjusted R2	Hostility		Duration		Cooperation	
			b1	s1	b2	s2	b3	s3
Arab states	.309	.285	-0.603	.000	0.981	.671	-0.416	.534
Israel	.613	.596	-1.181	.000	0.817	.722	0.333	.258
Both	.436	.420	-0.831	.000	6.192	.301	-0.228	.605
India	.225	.180	-0.861	.001	-1.930	.359	-1.908	.214
Pakistan	.476	.446	-0.964	0	-1.738	.342	0.381	.863
Both	.416	.394	-0.830	0	-4.012	.332	-0.341	.874
U.S.	.350	.210	-0.696	.026	0.091	.921	-0.047	.751
USSR	.703	.629	-1.111	.000	-0.491	.069	-0.030	.565
Both	.398	.328	-0.777	.000	-0.143	.828	-0.024	.718

durations between events? Why are the intensities of hostile events decreasing? Is it actually true that cooperative behavior plays no role in precrisis activity? These questions can be considered from two perspectives. First, the results obtained here could be a function of the definition of the relevant event sets. For example, in all three of the cases studied there were more international actors than are being used in the analysis. Incorporating the events for these additional actors could well change the analyses. Second, while the idea behind the event model may be valid—namely, its focus on events—its specification may be incorrect.

There are a variety of ways in which the event model might be modified, but modifications ought to take into account those results already obtained. The most surprising result is that the intensity of hostile events is decreasing. Although our modified event model indicated that cooperation did not play a role as incorporated in equations (5) and (6), perhaps the way in which cooperation enters the process was incorrectly specified and perhaps this error is additionally responsible for a negative parameter value on the hostility variable. Suppose that the cooperative events that transpire between successive hostile events are the cause for the decreasing intensities of hostility. Perhaps the hostile events are actually increasing the probability that the next hostile event will be more hostile, but this effect is contradicted by the intervening occurrence of cooperative events. Thus we could propose:

$$h(i + 1) - h(i) = a_1 h(i) + a_2 f(i') \qquad (7)$$

with the assumption that

$$a_1 > 0$$
$$a_2 < 0.$$

We could further propose that changes in the cooperative event sets are a relevant factor that must be explicitly postulated. It could be argued that changes in the intensity of cooperative event sets are a function of the intensity of previous cooperative behavior and the intensity of the previous hostile behavior:

$$f(i' + 1) - f(i') = b_1 f(i') + b_2 h(i) \qquad (8)$$

with the assumption that

$$b_1 > 0$$
$$b_2 < 0.$$

Finally, the durations between hostile event sets were not a function of the intensity of the previous hostile event, but perhaps they are a function of the intensity of the cooperative event set:

$$d(i+1) - d(i) = c_1 d(i) + c_2 f(i'). \tag{9}$$

While we would continue to expect

$$c_1 < 0,$$

since the durations are between hostile event sets, we might propose that

$$c_2 > 0$$

on the grounds that cooperative behavior should make subsequent hostile events less likely, i.e., it should increase the duration until the next hostile event.

The above model is a straightforward modification of the first event model and as such it does not include any consideration of the impact of durations between cooperative event sets. The relationship of durations between *hostile* event sets and durations between *cooperative* event sets is an important avenue for future research. It will, however, require a new set of definitions that permits the construction of a chronology of cooperative event sets that does not depend on the occurrence of hostile event sets and yet bears some time relationship to the occurrence of hostile events. This intriguing task is left for future research.

REFERENCES

Allan, Pierre. 1980. Diplomatic Time and Climate: A Formal Model. *Journal of Peace Science* 4, 2:133-50.

Azar, Edward; Bennett, James; and Sloan, Thomas. 1974. Steps Towards Forecasting International Interactions. *Peace Science Society (International) Papers* 23:27-68.

Bueno de Mesquita, Bruce. 1981. *The War Trap.* New Haven: Yale Univ. Press.

Burrowes, Robert, and Garrigo-Pico, Jose. 1974. The Road to the Six Day War: Relational Analysis of Conflict and Cooperation. *Peace Science Society (International) Papers* 22:47-74.

Holsti, Ole R.; North, Robert C.; and Brody, Richard A. 1968. Perception and Action in the 1914 Crisis. In *Quantative International Politics: Insights and Evidence,* J. David Singer (ed.), New York: Free Press, pp. 123-58.

Kaplan, Morton, 1957. *Systems and Process in International Politics.* New York: John Wiley and Sons.

Wilkenfeld, Jonathan; Lussier, Virginia Lee; and Tantinen, Dale. 1972. Conflict Interactions in the Middle East, 1949-1967. *J of Conflict Resolution* XVI, 2:135-54.

Zinnes, Dina A.; Hill, Barbara J.; Jones, David L.; and Majeski, Stephen J. 1982. Modeling Precrisis Interactions. In *New Dimensions in Political Science,* Judith Gillespie and Dina A. Zinnes, (eds.), Beverly Hills: Sage.

Manuscript Submission and Previous Publications

MANUSCRIPT SUBMISSION

The *Monograph Series in World Affairs,* published quarterly since 1963 by the Graduate School of International Studies, focuses on theoretic developments and research results dealing with contemporary problems of international relations. In treatment and scope, scholarly pieces that fall between journal and book length manuscripts are suitable. Thoughtful, relevant studies presented analytically in historical and social science frameworks are welcome. Statements of fact or opinion remain the responsibility of the authors alone and do not imply endorsement by the editors or publishers.

Submission: Send manuscripts in triplicate to Karen A. Feste, Editor, Monograph Series in World Affairs, Graduate School of International Studies, University of Denver, Denver, Colorado 80208. Manuscripts already published, scheduled for publication elsewhere, or simultaneously submitted to another journal are not acceptable. Manuscripts will be returned to authors only if accompanied, on submission, by a stamped, self-addressed envelope.

Abstract: Each manuscript must be summarized with a one to two page abstract indicating framework, setting, methodology, and findings.

Author Identification: On a separate page, specify manuscript title, full name and address of author(s), academic or other professional affiliations, and indicate to whom correspondence and galley proofs should be sent. A brief paragraph describing the author's research interest and recent publications should accompany the manuscript. Since manuscripts are sent out anonymously for evaluation, the author's name and affiliation should appear only on a separate covering sheet, as should all footnotes identifying the author.

Form: Manuscripts should be typed double-spaced (including footnotes), with footnotes, references, tables, charts, and figures on separate pages. Authors should follow the Chicago *Manual of Style* except as noted below regarding references. Footnotes should be numbered by chapter. Excessive footnoting should be avoided. Tables, figures, and charts should be mentioned in the text, numbered with Arabic numerals, and given a brief, descriptive title. A guideline should be inserted to indicate their appropriate place in the text.

References: In the text: All source references are to be identified at the appropriate point in the text by the last name of the author, year of publication, and pagination where needed. Identify subsequent citations of the same source in the same way as the first, not using *ibid., op. cit.,* or *loc. sit.* Examples: If author's name is in the text, follow it with year in parentheses [...Morcan, (1969)...]. If author's name is not in the text, insert, in parentheses, the last name and year, separated by a comma [...(Davidson, 1957)...]. Pagination follows year of publication after a colon [...(Budd, 1967:24)...]. Give both last names for dual authors; for more than two, use *et al.* If there is more than one reference to one author and year, distinguish them by letters added to the year [...(1977a)...].

In the Reference Section: The reference section must include all references cited in the text. The use of *et al.* is not acceptable; list the full name of all authors. The format for books: author, year of publication, title, place of publication, publisher. The format for journals: author, year of publication, title of article, name of periodical, volume, number, month, page.

Evaluations: Each manuscript is reviewed by the editor and at least two other readers. Almost always, two reviews are sought outside the University of Denver. General policy is to complete the evaluation process and communicate the editorial decision to the author within four months. Full referee reports are sent to the author. Anonymity of author and reviewer is preserved. Scholars who have furnished reviews of manuscripts during the year will be listed in the final issue of each volume.

Accepted Manuscripts: Manuscripts accepted for publication are subject to copy editing in our office. Edited versions (and later, page proofs) will be sent to the author for approval before materials are given to the printer. These must be returned within ten days. Due to prohibitive cost, substantial changes proposed at the page proof stage will be made at the discretion of the editors; or, alternatively, the cost of such changes will be billed to the author. Instructions for the preparation of camera-ready artwork will be forwarded to the author upon acceptance of the manuscript for publication. This artwork (tables, graphs, figures, photos) must be completed and approved before the production process will be initiated. Ten copies of the published monograph will be supplied free of charge to the senior author.

Permission Policy: To obtain permission to photocopy or to translate materials from the *Monograph Series,* please contact the editor.

Advertising: Current rates and specifications may be obtained by writing the managing editor.

Rates: Annual subscription: $24.00 domestic; $28.00 foreign. Write for our List of Publications brochure for single issue prices.

MONOGRAPH SERIES IN WORLD AFFAIRS
Publications

Volume 1, 1963-1964 Series

Rupert Emerson. *Political Modernization: The Single-Party System.*

Wendell Bell and Ivar Oxall. *Decisions of Nationhood: Political and Social Development in the British Caribbean.*

Volume 2, 1964-1965 Series

John C. Campbell. *The Middle East in the Muted Cold War.*

Dean G. Pruitt. *Problem Solving in the Department of State.*

James R. Scarritt. *Political Change in a Traditional African Clan: A Structural-Functional Analysis of the Nsits of Nigeria.*

Volume 3, 1965-1966 Series

Jack Citrin. *United Nations Peacekeeping Activities: A Case Study in Organizational Task Expansion.*

Ernst B. Haas and Philippe C. Schmitter. *The Politics of Economics in Latin American Regionalism: The Latin American Free Trade Association after Four Years of Operation* (out of print).

Taylor Cole. *The Canadian Bureaucracy and Federalism, 1947-1965.*

Arnold Rivkin. *Africa and the European Common Market: A Perspective.* (Revised Second Edition)

Volume 4, 1966-1967 Series

Edwin C. Hoyt. *National Policy and International Law: Case Studies from American Canal Policy.*

Bruce M. Russett and Carolyn C. Cooper. *Arms Control in Europe: Proposals and Political Constraints.*

Vincent Davis. *The Politics of Innovation: Patterns in Navy Cases.*

Yaroslav Bilinsky. *Changes in the Central Committee Communist Party of the Soviet Union, 1961-1966.*

Volume 5, 1967-1968 Series

Ernst B. Haas. *Collective Security and the Future International System.*

M. Donald Hancock. *Sweden: A Multiparty System in Transition?*

W.A.E. Skurnik, Editor, Rene Lemarchand, Kenneth W. Grundy and Charles F. Andrain. *African Political Thought: Lumumba, Nkrumah, and Toure.*

Volume 6, 1968-1969 Series

Frederick H. Gareau. *The Cold War 1947-1967: A Quantitative Study.*

Henderson B. Braddick. *Germany, Czechoslovakia, and the "Grand Alliance" in the May Crisis, 1938.*

Robert L. Friedheim. *Understanding the Debate on Ocean Resources.*

Richard L. Siegel. *Evaluating the Results of Foreign Policy: Soviet and American Efforts in India.*

Volume 7, 1969-1970 Series

Quincy Wright. *On Predicting International Relations, The Year 2000.*

James N. Rosenau. *Race in International Politics: A Dialogue in Five Parts.*

William S. Tuohy and Barry Ames. *Mexican University Students in Politics: Rebels without Allies?*

Karl H. Hoerning. *Secondary Modernization: Societal Changes of Newly Developing Nations—A Theoretical Essay in Comparative Sociology.*

Volume 8, 1970-1971 Series

Young W. Kihl. *Conflict Issues and International Civil Aviation: Three Cases* (out of print).

Morton Schwartz. *The "Motive Forces" of Soviet Foreign Policy, A Reappraisal.*

Joseph I. Coffey. *Deterrence in the 1970s* (out of print).

Edward Miles. *International Administration of Space Exploration and Exploitation.*

Volume 9, 1971-1972 Series

Edwin G. Corr. *The Political Process in Colombia.*

Shelton L. Williams. *Nuclear Nonproliferation in International Politics: The Japanese Case.*

Sue Ellen M. Charlton. *The French Left and European Integration.*

Volume 10, 1972-1973 Series

Robert W. Dean. *Nationalism and Political Change in Eastern Europe: The Slovak Question and the Czechoslovak Reform Movement.*

M. Donald Hancock. *The Bundeswehr and the National People's Army: A Comparative Study of German Civil-Military Polity.*

Louis Rene Beres. *The Management of World Power: A Theoretical Analysis.*

George A. Kourvetaris and Betty A. Dobratz. *Social Origins and Political Orientations of Officer Corps in a World Perspective.*

Volume 11, 1973-1974 Series

Waltraud Q. Morales. *Social Revolution: Theory and Historical Application.*

David O'Shea. *Education, the Social System, and Development.*

Robert H. Bates. *Patterns of Uneven Development: Causes and Consequences in Zambia.*

Robert L. Peterson. *Career Motivations of Administrators and Their Impact in the European Community.*

Volume 12, 1974-1975 Series

Craig Liske and Barry Rundquist. *The Politics of Weapons Procurement: The Role of Congress.*

Barry M. Schutz and Douglas Scott. *Natives and Settlers: A Comparative Analysis of the Politics of Opposition and Mobilization in Northern Ireland and Rhodesia.*

Vincent B. Khapoya. *The Politics of Decision: A Comparative Study of African Policy Toward the Liberation Movements.*

Louis Rene Beres. *Transforming World Politics: The National Roots of World Peace.*

Volume 13, 1975-1976 Series

Wayne S. Vucinich. *A Study in Social Survival: Katun in the Bileca Rudine.*

Jan F. Triska and Paul M. Johnson. *Political Development and Political Change in Eastern Europe: A Comparative Study.*

Louis L. Ortmayer. *Conflict, Compromise, and Conciliation: West German-Polish Normalization 1966-1976.*

James B. Bruce. *Politics of Soviet Policy Formation: Khrushchev's Innovative Policies in Education and Agriculture.*

Volume 14, 1976-1977 Series

Daniel J. O'Neil. *Three Perennial Themes of Anti-Colonialism: The Irish Case.*

Thomas Lobe. *United States National Security Policy and Aid to the Thailand Police.*

David F. Cusack. *Revolution and Reaction: The Internal and International Dynamics of Conflict and Confrontation in Chile.*

David F. Cusack. *The Death of Democracy and Revolution in Chile, 1970-1973.* Slide Show-Narrative Cassette (out of print).

Robert E. Harkavy. *Spectre of a Middle Eastern Holocaust: The Strategic and Diplomatic Implications of the Israeli Nuclear Weapons Program.*

Volume 15, 1977-1978 Series

Lewis W. Snider. *Arabesque: Untangling the Patterns of Conventional Arms Supply to Israel and the Arab States and the Implications for United States Policy on Supply of "Lethal" Weapons to Egypt.*

Bennett Ramberg. *The Seabed Arms Control Negotiations: A Study of Multilateral Arms Control Conference Diplomacy.*

Todd M. Sandler, William Loehr, and Jon T. Cauley. *The Political Economy of Public Goods and International Cooperation.*

Ronald M. Grant and E. Spencer Wellhofer, Editors. *Ethno-Nationalism, Multinational Corporations, and the Modern State.*

Volume 16, 1978-1979 Series

Sophia Peterson. *Sino-Soviet-American Relations: Conflict, Communication and Mutual Threat.*

Robert H. Donaldson. *The Soviet-Indian Alignment: Quest for Influence.*

Volume 17, 1979-1980 Series

Pat McGowan and Helen E. Purkitt. *Demystifying "National Character" in Black Africa: A Comparative Study of Culture and Foreign Policy Behavior.*

Theodore H. Cohn. *Canadian Food Aid: Domestic and Foreign Policy Implications.*

Robert A. Hoover. *Arms Control: The Interwar Naval Limitation Agreements.*

Lisa Robock Shaffer and Stephen M. Shaffer. *The Politics of International Cooperation: A Comparison of U.S. Experience in Space and in Security.*

Volume 18, 1980-1981 Series

Massiye Edwin Koloko. *The Manpower Approach to Planning: Theoretical Issues and Evidence from Zambia.*

Harry Eckstein. *The Natural History of Congruence Theory.*

P. Terrence Hopmann, Dina A. Zinnes, and J. David Singer, Eds. *Cumulation in International Relations Research.*

Philip A. Schrodt. *Preserving Arms Distributions in a Multi-Polar World: A Mathematical Study.*

Volume 19, 1981-1982 Series

Michael D. Ward. *Research Gaps in Alliance Dynamics.*

Theresa C. Smith. *Trojan Peace: Some Deterrence Propositions Tested.*

Roslyn L. Simowitz. *The Logical Consistency and Soundness of the Balance of Power Theory.*

Martin W. Sampson III. *International Policy Coordination: Issues in OPEC and EACM.*

Volume 20, 1982-1983 Series

John E. Turner, Vicki L. Templin, Roger W. Benjamin, Dong Suh Bark, Hoon Yu. *Community Development and Rational Choice: A Korean Study.*

Dina A. Zinnes, Ed. *Conflict Processes and the Breakdown of International Systems.* Merriam Seminar Series on Research Frontiers.

Conflict

All Warfare Short of War
Edited by George K. Tanham

This quarterly journal focuses on conflicts short of formal war, including guerrilla warfare, insurgency, revolution, and terrorism. Articles also cover non-physical conflicts, such as those of an economic, social, political, and psychological nature. Issues will attempt to address some of the less visible and less publicized conflicts occurring in the world today.

Selected Articles from the Fourth Volume of CONFLICT:

Issued Quarterly Volume 5 $60.00

Crane, Russak & Company, Inc.
3 East 44th Street, New York, N.Y. 10017, (212) 867-1490

CAIRO PAPERS IN SOCIAL SCIENCE
بحوث القاهرة فى العلوم الاجتماعية

The CAIRO PAPERS IN SOCIAL SCIENCE provides a medium for the dissemination of research in social, economic and political development conducted by visiting and local scholars working in Egypt and the Middle East. Produced at the American University in Cairo since 1977, CAIRO PAPERS has published more than 20 issues of collected articles and monographs on a variety of topics. Beginning January 1983, issues will appear on a quarterly basis. Future topics include:

> THE POLITICAL ECONOMY OF REVOLUTIONARY IRAN
> URBAN RESEARCH STRATEGIES FOR EGYPT
> THE HISTORY AND ROLE OF THE EGYPTIAN PRESS
> SOCIAL SECURITY AND THE FAMILY IN EGYPT
> THE NATIONALIZATION OF ARABIC AND ISLAMIC
>   EDUCATION IN EGYPT: DAR AL-ULUM AND AL-AZHAR
> NON-ALIGNMENT IN A CHANGING WORLD

In addition, we plan to publish a special index of survey research conducted by Egyptian research centers and agencies which will be offered at a discount rate to our subscribers.

****
NAME: INSTITUTION:

ADDRESS:

CITY: STATE OR COUNTRY:

VOLUME SIX ORDERS
        INDIVIDUAL (US $15 or L.E.8)   INSTITUTIONAL (US $25 or L.E.10)
                                    Please indicate if standing order:

BACK ORDERS
        SINGLE ISSUES (US $4 or L.E.3)   _____VOLUME 4 (US $15 or L.E.8)
Please indicate title and author:

Enclosed is a check or money order for_____payable to THE AMERICAN UNIVERSITY IN CAIRO (CAIRO PAPERS).

Signature or authorization:

****
Inquiries or orders originating in the   Those originating elsewhere should
USA should be sent to: be sent to:

CAIRO PAPERS IN SOCIAL SCIENCE   **CAIRO PAPERS IN SOCIAL SCIENCE**
American University in Cairo   **American University in Cairo**
866 U.N. Plaza   **P.O. Box 2511**
New York, N.Y. 10017   **Cairo, Egypt**

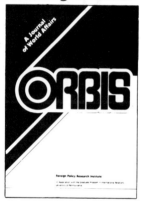

JOURNAL OF INTERNATIONAL AFFAIRS

Winter 1983   Volume 37/2

Largely an offspring of the colonial system and Western cultural mores, international law is being transformed as a result of the political and economic metamorphosis of the newly awakened Third World. What changes will occur?

THE POLITICS

OF

INTERNATIONAL

LAW

Published since 1947, the Journal has a readership in over 70 countries.

Subscription Rates:	One Year	Two Years	Three Years
Individual	$11.00	$21.00	$31.00
Institutions	$22.00	$43.00	$64.00

Foreign subscribers, except Canada, add $3.50 per year postage.

single issue price: $5.50

Mail all orders to: **Journal of International Affairs**

Box 4, International Affairs Building   •   Columbia University   •   New York, New York 10027

— At the forefront of facts and issues —

INTERNATIONAL STUDIES NOTES

of the International Studies Association

— a forum for conflicting views —

INTERNATIONAL STUDIES NOTES is published to provide a challenging *multidisciplinary* forum for exchange of research, curricular and program reports on international affairs. It is designed to serve teachers, scholars, practitioners, and others concerned with the international arena.

Recent and future topics include: terror; science, technology and development; classroom simulations; human rights; local-global links; gaps between policymakers and academics; contradictory approaches to international affairs; summaries/comments on professional meetings.

Recent contributors have included Norman D. Palmer, David P. Forsythe, James N. Roseneau, Robert C. North, and Rose Hayden.

— RECOMMEND A SUBSCRIPTION TO YOUR LIBRARIAN —

INTERNATIONAL STUDIES NOTES of the International Studies Association is published quarterly by the University of Nebraska-Lincoln and the University of Wyoming and is edited by Joan Wadlow and Leslie Duly.

Subscription Rates: One year $20.00; two years $36.00.

Send subscriptions to: Leslie Duly, 1223 Oldfather Hall, University of Nebraska-Lincoln, Lincoln, Nebraska 68588.

AFRICA TODAY

Inform your classes and your friends about Africa's most disputed territory:

Namibia

Take advantage of this special offer from Africa Today.

Two issues, including a special double issue, for only $4.00!
Special Double Issue Vol. 30, Nos. 1&2
(published 15 October, 1983)

Namibia and the West: Multinational Corporations and International Law
($3.00 separately)
and
Vol. 29, No. 1
(published 30 July, 1982)
Namibia, South Africa and the West
($2.50 separately)

or use these special bulk rates:

	30/1&2 only	plus 29/1
4-9 copies	$1.80 ea.	$2.50
10-19 copies	1.60 ea.	2.20
20 or more copies	1.45 ea.	2.00

Cash with order postage free. Postage extra on billed orders. All overseas orders postage additional 50¢ per copy surface, $2.00 per copy air mail.

- -

____I accept your special offer for the two issues of **Africa Today** on Namibia. Please send ____copies of 30/1&2 and 29/1.
____I wish to purchase____copies of 30/1&2 only.
My payment of $_____is enclosed.
Please bill me_____. I will pay the postal charges.

Name _____

Street Address_____

City _____ State_____Zip_____

Country_____(If outside the United States)
(Sorry. If you live outside the U.S. or Canada payment must accompany order. Be sure to include postal charges.)

FORO INTERNACIONAL

Revista trimestral publicada por El Colegio de México

Fundador: **Daniel Cosío Villegas**   Director: **Rafael Segovia**

vol. XXIV (2)   octubre-diciembre de 1983   núm. 94

ARTICULOS Y ENSAYOS

RESEÑAS DE LIBROS, LIBROS RECIBIDOS
Y REVISTA DE REVISTAS

FORO INTERNACIONAL 94

Adjunto cheque o giro bancario núm._____del banco
_____ a nombre de
El Colegio de México, A.C., por la cantidad de _____,
importe de mi suscripción por____año(s) a **Foro Internacional.**

Nombre_____
Dirección _____
_____ Ciudad_____
Estado _____ País _____
Código Postal_____ Tel. _____

Suscripción anual   México: 800 pesos   /   E.U.A., Canadá, centro y sur de
América; 25 U.S. Dls.   /   Otros países; 34 U.S. Dls.

Favor de enviar este cupón a **El Colegio de México**, Departamento de
Publicaciones, Camino al Ajusco 20, Col. Pedregal de Santa Teresa,
10740 México, D.F.

If you are interested in the study of politics
and government, you are invited to join

The Southern Political Science Association

MEMBERSHIP INCLUDES

The Journal of Politics

The Journal of Politics is a quarterly devoted to enriching and advancing
the knowledge of politics. Inside its pages all methods, positions, concep-
tualizations, and techniques are expounded by authors who know their
subjects and who back their ideas with careful research and positive schol-
arship. There is no bias in The Journal of Politics—toward theory,
American politics, or anything else. It is an open journal. Missing it is
missing an adventure into the character of political variety.

Upon receipt of this form you will begin a one-year membership in The Southern
Political Science Association, including a subscription to The Journal of Politics.

_____ Individual .... $ 17.00
_____ Student or Retired .... $ 10.00
_____ Institution .... $ 25.00
_____ Foreign Postage (additional) .... $ 5.50

Name_____

Address _____

_____

_____
                                            Zip Code

Please make check or money order payable to The Journal of Politics. Send to:

                 The Journal of Politics
                 University of Florida
                 Gainesville, FL, USA 32611

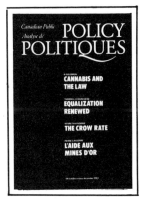

Book format and printing
by
DEPARTMENT OF GRAPHICS
University of Denver